IMAGES
of America

CASCADIAN HOTEL

IMAGES
of America

CASCADIAN HOTEL

Helen J. Knowles and L. Darlene Spargo

ARCADIA
PUBLISHING

Published by Arcadia Publishing
Charleston, South Carolina

Printed in the United States of America

Library of Congress Control Number: 2020931064

For all general information, please contact Arcadia Publishing:
Telephone 843-853-2070
Fax 843-853-0044
E-mail sales@arcadiapublishing.com
For customer service and orders:
Toll-Free 1-888-313-2665

Visit us on the Internet at www.arcadiapublishing.com

*For my partner John, the light in my life;
and, in memory of Jenny*

—Helen J. Knowles

*To my husband, James Spargo,
who has always been there*

—L. Darlene Spargo

CONTENTS

ACKNOWLEDGMENTS

It is a fortunate quirk of scholarly fate that Helen gathered too much material about the history of the Cascadian while conducting research for another book. That research provided her with more than was necessary to explain the role it played in the landmark 1937 US Supreme Court decision analyzed in *Making Minimum Wage: Elsie Parrish v. The West Coast Hotel Company* (to be published by the University of Oklahoma Press in 2021). Not one to let good research go to waste, she sought a publication venue for the additional material and found the perfect one in Arcadia's Images of America series. She also found the perfect coauthor in Darlene, a Wenatchee historian par excellence, who spent countless hours poring over genealogical records and microfilm of old newspapers. Darlene was an absolute joy to work with.

Darlene and Helen express their gratitude to the archives, libraries, and museums, and the owners of private collections of family photographs, who graciously assisted. Many images appear courtesy of the Wenatchee Valley Museum and Cultural Center (WVMCC) and the Manuscript, Archives & Special Collections Library at Washington State University (MASC-WSU). The courtesy line "HJK" denotes images from Helen's personal collection. The authors are particularly grateful to Paul Moseley, the current custodian of the Cascadian building, for taking us on tours and uncovering priceless artifacts illuminating so many aspects of the Cascadian's history.

The authors are also exceptionally grateful to Erin Vosgien, at Arcadia, for having faith in this project, and Angel Hisnanick for helping them navigate the production process.

Helen extends her thanks to her mother, Rae; to Toffee (who frequently donned his editor-in-chief cap) and his feline step-siblings Smokey, Clementine, and Faith; and Doc, the horse. Above all else, she expresses her love for John.

Helen (and John) would like to dedicate this book to Jenny, who was taken from this world far too soon. May she fly high as our guardian angel.

Darlene is grateful to Vera and Wyatt Henderson, who keep her imagination flowing by requesting an unending supply of spontaneous bedtime stories. She thanks Helen for expanding her world.

INTRODUCTION

As a movie camera rolled, capturing the moment for posterity, ground was broken at the construction site for the Cascadian Hotel on February 27, 1929. This would be the first skyscraper built in the town of Wenatchee in the North Central region of Washington State. Mayor E.J. Widby, Frederick M. Crollard (president of the chamber of commerce), and Nathan I. Neubauer (the head of the board of directors for the planned hotel) wielded the shovels at the ground-breaking ceremony. Financier Hyman Harris, a Wenatchee pioneer, had led the fundraising effort for the hotel, and financial backing for the project came from a Seattle-based investment firm owned by Grover C. Winn. Excavation took longer than expected with the discovery of oily sand and a shallow bed of coal sitting atop a layer of hard rock. Dynamite was used to clear the area, and excavation was completed on March 19.

General contractor A.D. Belanger was in charge of the project. The building of the 10-story hotel proceeded at an amazing pace. After the first two floors were poured, two floors a week were added. Work was held up for 10 days because of equipment failure at the pit, or the hotel would have been completed even more quickly. According to an interview with the *Wenatchee Daily World*, Long's Storage and Transfer Company trucks hauled "390,000 feet lumber; 474,000 sacks of cement; 84 yards of sand; 44,896 pounds of tile; 151,900 pounds miscellaneous freight; 190,000 pounds plumbing fixtures; 39,647 pounds electrical apparatus; 100,757 pounds of radiators and steam fittings, which includes boilers; 1,023,910 pounds of brick; 1,072,070 pounds steel; 123 tons of plaster." While bricklayers worked outside, all other trades were busy inside. The hotel was erected in just over five months, opening on August 9, 1929. An expansion in 1930 gave the hotel a total of 200 rooms and apartments.

Architect Frank Mahon's Art Deco design was evident throughout the building, including lighting fixtures, furniture, and door hardware. The *Daily World* newspaper described the brick-clad concrete structure as having "variegated buff-colored brick from curb to crest with brilliant futuristic terra cotta ornamentations at the top." The flooring in the lobby and coffee shop was terrazzo and the fixtures mahogany. The Cascadian was a first-class facility that had pride of place in Wenatchee's downtown.

Not to be outdone in speed, the Neubauer Building Company built Bennett's Cascadian Super-Parking garage across the street in 60 days. The garage contained parking space for 200 cars, fuel pumps, lube, and tire services. As a nod to hotel guests, a dog kennel was built in the basement and open for day or overnight care.

The construction of the Cascadian was a boon to local Wenatchee businesses. The construction trades were not the only ones to benefit. The E.T. Pybus Company built and installed the fire escapes and building marquees. A 20-man crew from Wenatchee Paint and Glass painted the interior, and Betty Morrison and C. W. Dam were the decorators. The Wenatchee Furniture Company provided the beds, mattresses and box springs, dressers, desks, general furniture, and all carpets and linings.

With a view to becoming the best small hotel in the Pacific Northwest, the Cascadian was built with a state-of-the-art kitchen, soundproof rooms, air conditioning, and phones in every room. Ray W. Clark was hired as the manager. He began his hotel career as a 14-year-old boy at the Oregon Hotel in Portland. Clark shared his goals for the Cascadian in an interview with the *Daily World*: "Service, Smiles, Good Food, Quiet Rest Assured; Personal touch put into service." One special feature offered guests were "Longfellow" rooms: five rooms containing beds seven feet long to accommodate tall guests. Clark believed good service and good advertising would bring tourists to the Wenatchee Valley. He arranged for four tour companies from New York and the East Coast to advertise the valley. In an effort to bring conventions to town, the Cascadian planned to spend $20,000 in advertising in the first year. Those plans were obviously affected by the coming of the Great Depression.

During World War II and the Cold War, volunteers in defense of North America served as ground observers on top of the Cascadian Hotel, spotting airplanes. Jackie Newell Smart was one of those volunteers.

The Cascadian continued to welcome guests and conventions, club meetings, and social events, but times were changing. The advent of interstate highways and inexpensive automobile transportation changed the way people traveled. Large hotels did not meet the requirements of vacationing families. Motels now dotted the landscape. In an attempt to move with the times, a motor lodge with a pool was added to the back of the Cascadian in the early 1960s.

This was an attempt to save a hotel that had been steadily losing money since the mid-1950s. Wilfred Woods, and Jerry Barash, manager of the Columbia Hotel, formed a corporation with Jim Arneil, Vern Stockwell, Ed Hansen, Jim Trucano, Clair Van Divort, and Bob Woods in order to purchase the Cascadian in 1962. Van Divort added a new banquet room to the hotel, and Barash took over as manager. Their attempt to return the hotel to a profitable state proved to be impossible. The corporation dissolved after two years, and Balanced Investments became the owner in 1965. James D. Ward, as Cascadian Enterprises, purchased the Cascadian in 1967, giving the hotel one last chance at survival. Ward was a native of Wenatchee, the son of Ossie and Nellie Morgan Ward. He worked in food services as a student at Seattle University. This led to work in the Frye and Olympic Hotels. He became a supervisor of Jorgenson's restaurants and, in 1946, opened the Mocha Shop in Seattle. He purchased the Jorgenson chain in 1950. Ward was the owner of Pancho's Restaurant, 13 Coins, Carriage Inn, the Sir Loin Inn, and opened the El Gaucho Restaurant in 1953 in Seattle. Before purchasing the Cascadian Hotel, he owned the Windsor Hotel and the Tyee Motor Inn in Olympia. Despite his vast experience, Ward was unable to save the Cascadian and dissolved Cascadian Enterprises in 1969. The Cascadian finally closed its doors on July 19, 1971. When the hotel closed, the Motor Inn was spun off and turned into condominiums and rented to the general public.

On Friday February 23, 1973, people gathered at Colonel Jim's Gold Creek Auction House, in Woodinville, in order to bid on items from the Cascadian, including, as the *Daily World* reported, "200 to 300 pillows, countless blankets and sheets, lamps, night stands and other furniture." Nine months later, the main Cascadian building, newly renovated, opened as government-subsidized housing for elders and the disabled. Tryg Fortun acquired the building in 2004. It continues to be used as government-subsidized housing, although at the end of 2020, when the government contract ends, the rent for the apartments will change to market-rate. The Cascadian remains the tallest structure in town, a defining element of the Wenatchee landscape, and a permanent reminder of its rich history.

During the 1970s, many storefronts in downtown Wenatchee underwent dramatic reconfigurations. The Cascadian, however, was spared most of these facial ignominies, and in 2008 the National Register of Historic Places approved designating eight blocks as the Downtown Wenatchee National Historic Register District, with all the architectural protections that such a label brings. The Cascadian and the surrounding buildings were safe, ensuring that future generations will understand what Tracy Warner, a *Wenatchee World* reporter, meant when he wrote: "[w]hen we look at the old hotel that still dominates our skyline, we see a place of history."

One

EARLY WENATCHEE

Wenatchee's humble beginnings were a simple log trading post near the Wenatchee River built by Dan and Frank Freer around 1870. Phillip Miller later became a partner and planted apple trees in 1872. In 1891, the population was 108, but within a year that grew to 300 because of the Great Northern Railway's decision to build its line through the valley and across Stevens Pass to Seattle. The Wenatchee Development Company surveyed and platted the present site of Wenatchee. After papers were filed in May 1892, lots were offered for sale, and within five days $100,000 worth of property was sold. Wenatchee now had access to markets and, by 1902, was calling itself the "Apple Capital of the World."

The influx of 4,000 railroad workers created an immediate demand for housing. N.N. Brown built the first hotel in 1892. The roof and sides of the two-story building were covered with tarpaper held on by batting. All of the building materials and furnishings had to be conveyed over the mountains by wagon from Ellensburg. Coal lamps or tallow candles lighted the rooms, and horses hauled water in.

The Bell Hotel, the second hotel in town, was the largest in North Central Washington, although Wenatchee's population only numbered between 400 and 500. The entire population turned out to celebrate the grand opening on the Fourth of July 1895.

By 1906, there were 3,500 residents. Driven by Rufus Woods and the *Wenatchee Daily World* newspaper, a rudimentary sewer system was installed in 1909 that drained into the Columbia River. Main streets were graded and oiled, board sidewalks replaced with cement, and electric streetlights installed. Besides the Bell and Watson Hotels, there were several small hotels in operation: the Hotel Roosevelt with 15 rooms, and the Park Hotel, Central House, Columbia Hotel, Howard Hotel, and Cottage House. In the late 1920s, the population reached 11,627, and the time was right for the building of a premier hotel. The opening of the Cascadian in 1929 added to Wenatchee's prestige as a forward-looking city with a strong agricultural economy.

This photograph shows the Charles Kyle Framing Shop and sewing machine store next door to the original Wenatchee Hotel. Board sidewalks lined the dirt streets. The image dates to approximately 1905, at a time of extensive growth for this pioneer town. The population jumped from approximately 450 in 1900 to over 4,000 in 1910. (Courtesy of WVMCC.)

L.D. Lindsley took this photograph of the exterior of the new Wenatchee Hotel in 1911. The stagecoach and livery stable to the right of the hotel did a thriving business. The new Wenatchee Hotel was opened in 1910 and closed over half a century later in 1965. (Courtesy of WVMCC.)

1119 Hotel Wenatchee, Wenatchee, Washington

The new Wenatchee Hotel boasted 67 rooms, with 32 having private baths. Every room faced outside, giving good light, ventilation, and a view. A distinctive feature of the Wenatchee Hotel was its rooftop garden on the second floor, with a number of guest rooms facing the garden. Phone service was available in every room, thanks to an in-house switchboard in the basement. This postcard was sent from the Wenatchee Hotel on July 21, 1911. "Will" had spent two weeks camping and fishing in the area with a friend. He would have had a comfortable room but no air conditioning. He notes that it was 106 degrees in the shade. (Both, courtesy of HJK.)

Wenatchee Ave., North, Wenatchee, Wash.

This street view shows Wenatchee Avenue before the many improvements made in 1909, when Wenatchee Avenue was leveled and oiled, electric street lights installed, cement sidewalks poured, and a rudimentary sewage system was built. A fire that July destroyed a block of wooden buildings. They were rebuilt with stone and brick. (Courtesy of HJK.)

The Way we Raise Them in
WENATCHEE, WASH.

M. L. Oakes produced a series of exaggerated real-photo postcards in the early 1900s. This 1907 card is an excellent example of Wenatchee advertising for their claims of being the "The Home of the Big Red Apple, Where Dollars Grow on Trees" and in 1902, "Apple Capital of the World." The first shipment of apples by rail to Seattle took place in 1901. (Courtesy of HJK.)

13

The Howard Hotel was a small hotel that followed the European Plan, which meant that no meals were served at the hotel. As with many of the early hotels, businesses occupied the first floor. The Toggery tailoring shop was located there in 1906. A gentleman has his trunk on the sidewalk at the hotel entrance. (Courtesy of WVMCC.)

The Clark Hotel was located on the corner of Wenatchee and Kittitas Streets and built in 1893. It became the first Chelan County Courthouse in 1900 and served in that capacity until the current courthouse was built in 1924. It reopened as the Doneen Hotel in 1929 (the same year that the Cascadian was constructed and opened). (Courtesy of WVMCC.)

The Bell Hotel went through several owners. The Bells sold to George Stetson, for $13,000, who changed the name to the Great Northern Hotel. N.N. Brown purchased the hotel in 1912, changing its name to the Elberta, after the famous Elberta peach. He added a new dining room. The Elberta was closed in 1943 and torn down in 1951. (Courtesy of WVMCC.)

Besides the Clark and Bell Hotels, there were several small hotels in operation in Wenatchee by 1906. The Hotel Roosevelt was equipped with 15 rooms; additionally, there were the Park Hotel, Central House, the first Columbia Hotel, Howard Hotel, and Cottage House. The original, small Columbia Hotel pictured here was built in 1902 and was located at 14 South Mission. It had a home-like atmosphere. (Courtesy of WVMCC.)

An Ellis real-photo postcard, this scene was shot by either John Boyd Ellis or his son Clifford C. Ellis. The Ellis Postcard Company produced around 5,000 different postcards. This one captured the original Penney's Department Store. Fire destroyed the store around 1962. Miller's Department Store, in the Griggs Building (founded by Steamboat Captain Alexander Griggs), is visible to the right of the Cascadian. (Courtesy of HJK.)

Eagle Transfer delivered this carload of hood rubbers to the Golden Rule Mercantile Company, which occupied part of the Elman Hotel Building. Still in operation, Eagle Livery and Transfer began business in 1903. It hauled the mail and freight from the train depot, carried baggage and passengers, and watered the dusty streets. (Courtesy of WVMCC.)

Columbia Hotel-Wenatchee Wash-   2-35A

The first Columbia Hotel was built in 1906 by Emil Miller and originally named the Chewawa. It was the first modern hotel in Wenatchee. For a time, it housed the Golden Rule Store, the eighth store in a chain founded by J.C. Penney. Miller leased it to E.L. Mann, who renamed it the Elman Hotel. The hotel boasted in 1930 that it had 200 strictly modern rooms "artificially cooled for your comfort" and offered "unexcelled service at moderate rates, with special rates for permanent guests." Their motto was, "We are personally responsible for your comfort." The Columbia is best remembered for its Kiltie Room, the center of a vibrant music scene, hosting nationally known pop and country music stars. (Courtesy of HJK.)

COLUMBIA HOTEL   WENATCHEE, WN.   'VI' A25.

Simmer's photograph of the Columbia Hotel captures the massive size of the building. Emil Miller added a third floor before he leased the hotel to E.L. Mann, who changed the name to the Elman Hotel. In 1926, A.G. Black extended the building 50 feet at the cost of $200,000 and renamed it the Columbia Hotel. It anchored the south end of Wenatchee Avenue while the Cascadian, after its construction in 1929, anchored the north end. The Columbia was closed by 1977. When it was torn down, it was replaced by Centennial Park. (Above, courtesy of WVMCC; below, courtesy of HJK.)

The Olympia Hotel was constructed in 1908 by J.M. Duffy, a sales agent of the Olympia Brewing Company and operator of Duffy's Saloon, just up the street. The 40-room hotel was built with the most modern fire safety measures available. The hotel closed in 1969. (Courtesy of HJK.)

Seen here in 1911, the Gem Theater was located on the first floor of the Olympia Hotel until it moved to the Griggs Building in 1914. Numerous businesses occupied the main floor over the years, including a hat store, cigar store, and Pay Less Drugs. The hotel closed in 1969, and the building was converted to commercial use. (Courtesy of WVMCC.)

Hotel Del Mundo (translation: "of the world") seems a grandiose name for this small hotel that was located on Mission Street in Wenatchee. The hotel was located next door to the office of the *Wenatchee Daily World* newspaper, which began servicing the region in 1905. This photograph of the Hotel Del Mundo was taken in 1911. (Courtesy of WVMCC.)

Arthur G. Simmer captured this image of the front view of the Hotel Chelan building at 8 Orondo Avenue, Wenatchee. The Chelan Pool Hall and the Chelan Café occupied the ground floor with the lobby located upstairs. Displayed in the windows of the building are advertisements for tobacco products and promotional material for an upcoming boxing event. (Courtesy of WVMCC.)

WENATCHEE, WASH., APPLE CAPITAL OF THE WORLD

The Great Northern Railway, as part of its "Scenes along the Great Northern Railway" series, published this c. 1930s postcard. The postcard features a photograph taken by Arthur G. Simmer. Wenatchee's fame as Apple Capital of the World first arose following successful shipments of apples to Seattle in 1901 and 1902. (Courtesy of HJK.)

In 1923, the Wenatchee Apple Blossom Festival was four years old. Today, as then, the local schools march in the Grand Parade held on the first Saturday of May. The two-week festival includes a children's parade, music, art, carnivals, craft fairs, athletic events, and car shows. Dian Ulrich, "Miss Western Hotels," rode on the Cascadian Hotel float in the 1960 Apple Blossom Parade. (Courtesy of WVMCC.)

APPLE BLOSSOM FESTIVAL
WENATCHEE 1923

In 1935, a group of Matanuska colonists from Alaska stopped in Wenatchee during their train trip to Seattle. In typical Apple Capital style, a salesman selling Skookum Brand apples and Aplets confectionary from his cart greeted them at the edge of the railroad tracks. (Courtesy of the Museum of History and Industry, *Seattle Post-Intelligencer* Collection, 1986.5.5463.2.)

Students give the Wenatchee apple sign a cleaning around 1960. Wenatchee began calling itself the Apple Capital of the World in 1902. The sign eventually had to be taken down, but Wenatchee citizens wanted a new one. They voted on the design and raised funds, and Graybeal Signs was chosen to create new signage. Since 2007, a smaller neon apple sign welcomes visitors. (Courtesy of WVMCC.)

Taken in the 1940s, this photograph of Wenatchee's renowned Ohme Gardens shows the Columbia River and a sparsely developed Wenatchee Valley below. When Herman and Ruth Ohme began their garden in 1929 (the same year the Cascadian Hotel opened) on nine acres of scrubby, rocky bluff overlooking the Columbia, they never imagined it would become the extensive public alpine garden it is today. (Courtesy of WVMCC.)

Framed by an orchard in full bloom, Saddle Rock rises 2,000 feet above the Wenatchee Valley. The mountain, with its weathered rock towers, is a Wenatchee landmark. Native American legend tells of Black Bear and Grizzly Bear constantly bickering until one day, when Coyote turned them both to stone, forming the saddle. Thousands climb the mountain every year for the panoramic view. (Courtesy of WVMCC.)

Two

Building the Cascadian Hotel

The Wenatchee City Council gave its formal blessing to the Cascadian early in 1929 after a number of prominent local residents pledged to purchase $50,000 in preferred stock from the hotel's operating company, the West Coast Hotel Company. A ground-breaking ceremony was held on February 27, presided over by the mayor of Wenatchee, the president of the chamber of commerce, and the head of the board of directors for the planned hotel. The hotel replaced the Browne and Murray Service Station at the corner of North Wenatchee Avenue and First Street. By April, the building finally had a name. After much speculation and a large number of suggestions, the investors settled upon the Cascadian.

Built at a cost of $500,000, the 10-story Cascadian, an impressive mixture of Art Moderne and Beaux Art styles, was the tallest building in town (as it is to this day). It featured cutting-edge technology, including a state-of-the-art air conditioning system, a rare feature for hotels built at this time in America.

Care was taken to use the services of local merchants to decorate and furnish the building, including the 133 guest rooms, coffee shop, and social hall. The human spider that scaled the façade of the Cascadian was the featured attraction of the formal opening on August 9. Shielding their eyes from the summer sun, the town's residents craned their necks for a better view of the gravity-defying attraction. Hundreds of sweltering onlookers marveled at the spider's ability to ascend the 10 stories effortlessly and seemingly immune to the effects of the 98-degree heat. When the stunt reached its spectacular climax—with the spider performing a handstand on the flagpole, 127 feet up—it drew whoops of terrified excitement. The festivities were accompanied by music courtesy of the Washington State Band and the American Legion drum and bugle corps, who performed at the ceremony for over an hour. The *Hotel News of the West* magazine described the Cascadian as "a success from the day it opened."

Grover C. Winn was the owner of the Seattle-based investment firm that backed the development of the Cascadian. Winn received his law degree from the University of Washington in 1910. He was a member of the Alaska Territorial House of Representatives from 1929 to 1932, serving as speaker from 1931 to 1932. (Courtesy of Alaska State Library.)

CASCADIAN HOTEL-WENATCHEE, WN VI A21

Ground was broken on February 27, 1929, for the $600,000 Cascadian Hotel, and it was officially opened on August 9, 1929. The opening ceremony featured a human spider who scaled the building's façade, then completed a handstand on the flagpole, 127 feet up. The hotel proudly proclaimed that it was fireproof and air-cooled and offered reasonable rates beginning at $2 a night. (Courtesy of HJK.)

Scaffolding surrounds the Cascadian as it was being built in 1929. The longer view of the construction is looking down First Street toward Wenatchee Avenue. Bob Dupar's family took over the hotel in 1930 when local investors could not pay the construction bills. He wrote in a letter to the *Wenatchee Daily World*: "Dad and uncle took the lead in getting the hotel operating and went down the street to Tom Polison and asked him how to figure the menu prices in his restaurant. 'How much do you charge for ham and eggs?' Tom told them not to worry about it. The printer up the street had already printed menus with the prices already printed on them." Dupar became the Cascadian's manager in 1954. (Both, courtesy of WVMCC.)

Looking east from the roof of the Cascadian building provides an impressive view of both the railroad tracks and the mighty Columbia River, two forms of transportation that proved central to the establishment and growth of Wenatchee. It also affords a close-up view of the Art Deco features atop the building. (Courtesy of HJK.)

In April 1929, the *Wenatchee Daily World* reported that "after much speculation," the new hotel finally had a name. *Hotel Monthly* magazine contributed to that "speculation," suggesting "the Clark Hotel, in honor of . . . Wenatchee pioneer" W.T. Clark, who is pictured here. Although Clark did not come to Wenatchee until 1902, he is widely regarded as "the Father of Wenatchee." (Courtesy of WVMCC.)

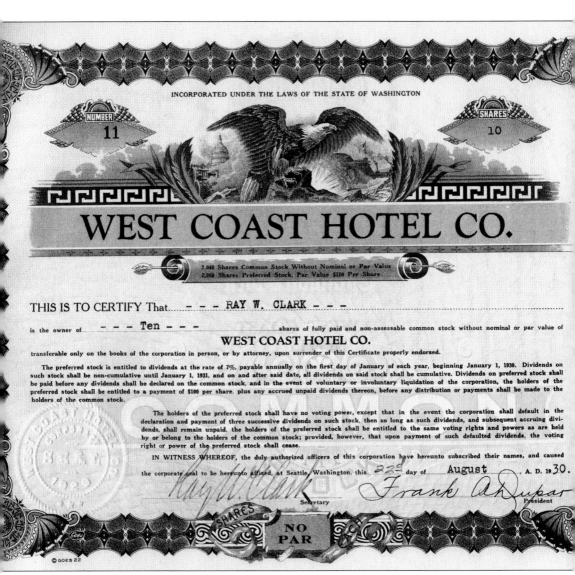

INCORPORATED UNDER THE LAWS OF THE STATE OF WASHINGTON

NUMBER 11

SHARES 10

WEST COAST HOTEL CO.

2,000 Shares Common Stock Without Nominal or Par Value
2,000 Shares Preferred Stock, Par Value $100 Per Share

THIS IS TO CERTIFY That _ _ _ RAY W. CLARK _ _ _

is the owner of _ _ _ Ten _ _ _ shares of fully paid and non-assessable common stock without nominal or par value of

WEST COAST HOTEL CO.

transferable only on the books of the corporation in person, or by attorney, upon surrender of this Certificate properly endorsed.

The preferred stock is entitled to dividends at the rate of 7%, payable annually on the first day of January of each year, beginning January 1, 1930. Dividends on such stock shall be non-cumulative until January 1, 1931, and on and after said date, all dividends on said stock shall be cumulative. Dividends on preferred stock shall be paid before any dividends shall be declared on the common stock, and in the event of voluntary or involuntary liquidation of the corporation, the holders of the preferred stock shall be entitled to a payment of $100 per share, plus any accrued unpaid dividends thereon, before any distribution or payments shall be made to the holders of the common stock.

The holders of the preferred stock shall have no voting power, except that in the event the corporation shall default in the declaration and payment of three successive dividends on such stock, then so long as such dividends, and subsequent accruing dividends, shall remain unpaid, the holders of the preferred stock shall be entitled to the same voting rights and powers as are held by or belong to the holders of the common stock; provided, however, that upon payment of such defaulted dividends, the voting right or power of the preferred stock shall cease.

IN WITNESS WHEREOF, the duly authorized officers of this corporation have hereunto subscribed their names, and caused the corporate seal to be hereunto affixed, at Seattle, Washington, this 22d day of August, A. D. 19 30.

Ray W. Clark
Secretary

Frank A Dupar
President

NO PAR

© GOES 22

In 1929, the Pacific Northwest hotelier Ray W. Clark was hired to be the Cascadian's first manager. He also became the secretary of the West Coast Hotel Company. This photograph shows the certificate for preferred stock in that company, which Clark was given in August 1930. Other members of the company's executive board and prominent residents of Wenatchee also held such stock. (Courtesy of MASC-WSU.)

When the Cascadian was furnished in 1929, an emphasis was placed on buying local—very local, in fact. Much of the furniture was purchased from the Wenatchee Furniture Company, which was located just down the street at 19 North Wenatchee Avenue—seen on the right-hand side of the thoroughfare in this photograph. (Courtesy of the Washington State Historical Society, Tacoma, image 1988.40.2.)

As Ray Clark, the Cascadian's manager, explained in a 1934 article in *Hotel Monthly*, he had finally "hit upon an idea which" would "bring a great deal of favorable comment" to the hotel. From the famed Shenango China Company in New Castle, Pennsylvania, he commissioned hand-painted china adorned with a "Delicious" apple design. Guests would eat from ware decorated with a bright red apple and bright green leaves; deliberately, for the plates, saucers, and cups, an Inca Ware style was chosen that eschewed the standard white hotel background in favor of a "dark cream." These dishes are striking in their appearance and no doubt served as an effective reminder to the diner that they were eating in the apple city. (Both, courtesy of MASC-WSU.)

On August 6, 1929, craftsmen were feverishly putting the finishing touches on the Cascadian because Ray Clark had guaranteed 33 local dealers and salesmen of Crosley & Amrad radio sets that the hotel would be ready to accommodate them at a banquet hosted by Harper-McGee, Inc., a Seattle-based radio distribution and records sales company. Clark kept his word. These radiomen were the first guests to dine at the Cascadian. Powel Crosley Jr. (left) of the Crosley Radio Corp., is pictured above in 1936 with Anning S. Prall, the chairman of the Federal Communications Commission and, below, with his 1938 radio set and company mascot, the "Crosley Pup" (Above, courtesy of the Library of Congress; right, courtesy of the Powel Crosley, J. Collection, Ohio History Connection, image AL02677.)

The Kelvinator Corporation had its roots in 1914 with Buick executives Edmund J. Copeland and Arnold H. Goss. In 1925, it produced the industry's first self-contained electric home refrigerator. The Copeland refrigerator was the top of the line, and the Cascadian had three units plus a pantry box. (Courtesy of Alamy.)

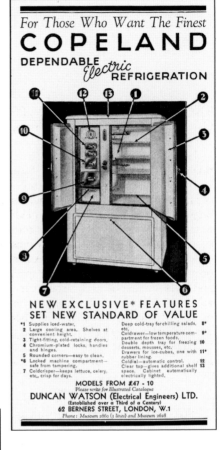

Walter Raymond, of Raymond & Whitcomb Travel Agency of Boston, Massachusetts, held a contest with the winner receiving a trip from Boston to Wenatchee to be the first guest to sign the register of the newly completed Cascadian Hotel. He eventually built the fabulous Raymond Hotel in Pasadena, California. Guests included Pres. Theodore Roosevelt and Charlie Chaplin. (Courtesy of the South Pasadena Public Library.)

The pricing structure decided upon for the Cascadian's coffee shop when it first opened in 1929 was redundant by 1933. This is because in 1933, in Washington State, the average taxpayer's net annual income was 50 percent less than it had been in 1929. Within weeks of Franklin Delano Roosevelt's inauguration on March 4, 1933, the Cascadian made plans to try and bring more diners to its coffee shop by capitalizing upon the new president's concept of a "New Deal" for the American people. For several months in the spring and early summer of 1933, a special menu appeared. Although other, slightly cheaper meals (including the "Bargain Luncheon") were available, they were not as good value for money as the headlining "New Deal Luncheon." (Both, courtesy of MASC-WSU.)

CASCADIAN COFFEE SHOP
MONDAY, JUNE 19, 1933.

45¢ "THE NEW DEAL LUNCHEON" 45¢
VEGETABLE SOUP JARDINERE
BAKED PORK CHOP, COUNTRY GRAVY
STEAMED FINNAN HADDIE
CHOPPED VEGETABLE SALAD
POTATOES   VEGETABLE
ROLLS   BUTTER
CHOICE OF PIES, ICE CREAM OR SHERBET
COFFEE, TEA, MILK OR BUTTERMILK.
+++++

40c   40c
BRIE-DENZER CHEESE SANDWICH WITH
WALDORF SALAD, COFFEE

40c   DUTCH PLATE   40c
+++++

DESSERTS
(NOT INCLUDED IN ABOVE LUNCHEON SPECIAL)
APPLE, FRESH RHUBARB OR CHOCOLATE PIE   10c
CAKE   -   -   -   10c
ICE CREAM OR SHERBET   -   -   10c
+++++

COLD SURPRISE PLATE   -   -   - 40c

+++++

35c   BARGAIN LUNCHEON   35c

LAMB STEW WITH VEGETABLES
POTATOES   SLICED TOMATOES
ROLLS
RICE PUDDING
COFFEE, TEA, MILK OR BUTTERMILK.

BLUE RIBBON, HAMMS, SCHLITZ & BLATZ
BEER, 20c PINT, DRAUGHT BEER 10c GLASS

CASCADIAN COFFEE SHOP
MONDAY, JULY 17, 1933.

45¢ "THE NEW DEAL LUNCHEON" 45¢
TOMATO MACARONI SOUP
BOILED BEEF, HORSERADISH SAUCE
POACHED HALIBUT, CHEESE SAUCE
BLUE GOOSE VEGETABLE PLATE
POTATOES   VEGETABLE
ROLLS   BUTTER
CHOICE OF PIES, ICE CREAM OR SHERBET
COFFEE, TEA, MILK OR BUTTERMILK,
+++++

40c   SPRING SPECIAL   40c
FRIED BANANAS SERVED WITH CRISP
BACON AND FRIED APPLES
ROLL   COFFEE

DESSERTS
(NOT INCLUDED IN ABOVE LUNCHEON SPECIAL)
APPLE, FRESH APRICOT PIE   10c
STEWED CHERRIES AND GINGER COOKIE   10c
CAKE   ,   -   -   -   10c
ICE CREAM OR SHERBET   -   -   10c
+++++

COLD SURPRISE PLATE   -   -   - 40c

+++++

35c   BARGAIN LUNCHEON   35c

BAKED MEAT LOAF
COLE SLAW   POTATOES
ROLLS
FRESH RASPBERRY TAPIOCA
COFFEE, TEA, MILK OR BUTTERMILK.

BLUE RIBBON, HAMMS, SCHLITZ & BLATZ
BEER, 20c PINT, DRAUGHT BEER 10c GLASS

BREAKFAST SPECIALS

1

ORANGE JUICE WITH DOLLAR WHEAT CAKES   50c
AND RASHER OF HAM OR BACON AND
(1) EGG   COFFEE

2

WENATCHEE BAKED APPLE AND CREAM   25c
TOAST OR HOT MUFFINS   (1) CUP COFFEE

3

ORANGE JUICE OR FRUIT IN SEASON   50c
(2) BOILED EGGS   TOAST   COFFEE

4

WAFFLE OR HOT CAKES STRIPPED   40c
WITH BACON OR HAM   COFFEE

5

BAKED APPLE OR TOMATO JUICE WITH   35c
WAFFLE OR HOT CAKES, AND   COFFEE

6

CEREAL AND CREAM. TOAST, (1)CUP COFFEE   25c

7

STRAWBERRIES AND CREAM   35c
TOAST   COFFEE

8

SOUR DOUGH HOT CAKES   COFFEE   25c

9

FRUIT IN SEASON OR CEREAL WITH CREAM   65c
WITH HAM OR BACON AND EGGS OR BREAKFAST STEAK
FRIED POTATOES   TOAST   COFFEE

This is an example of one of the "breakfast specials" menus offered by the Cascadian's coffee shop. From 1933, this particular menu shows two ways in which the coffee shop sought to attract customers. First, prices were kept low to appeal to local residents as well as the hotel's guests. Second, several of the meals featured local produce, such as Wenatchee baked apples. (Courtesy of MASC-WSU.)

Pres. Herbert Hoover and soon-to-be-president Franklin D. Roosevelt are seen here riding to Roosevelt's inauguration in Washington, DC, on March 4, 1933. The Great Depression hit the nation's hotels hard—80 percent were in receivership by 1935. Roosevelt's New Deal slowly but surely reinvigorated the country's economy and provided a much-need commercial boost for hotels, including the Cascadian, which had managed to survive during the early 1930s.

This is the cover of the souvenir program and menu card created for the Cascadian's "Frolic" on New Year's Eve 1934–1935. The event featured entertainment provided by Chuck Rubyn and the Hotel Cascadian Orchestra, and included "Tapping in the New Year by Lois Brown" and a performance by "'The Boogyman'"—an "Unknown Blackfaced Comedian." Food offerings included local fare, such as roast Washington turkey. (Courtesy of MASC-WSU.)

The back of this postcard states that the Cascadian Hotel and Motor Inn had "164 rooms, 24 Cabanas, Heated Pool, TV, and Apple Box Room." It also once housed a radio station. Wenatchee's first radio station, KPQ, began operating in December 1929, from a studio on the 10th floor. The transmitting antenna wire ran out of a window, across First Street, and to the roof of the hotel garage. (Courtesy of HJK.)

A history of broadcasting in the Pacific Northwest would be incomplete without discussion of (Lafayette) Rogan Jones, affectionately known to his family as "Paddy." As David Richardson writes in his book *Puget Sounds*, Jones had "an almost visionary urge to pioneer" and succeeded by "keep[ing] his brains busy and his checkbook idle." Jones acquired his first radio station, KXRO, in 1928. In 1929, he acquired KPQ in Wenatchee, installing studios in a suite of the Cascadian. Above, Jones, together with Hoyt Wertz (Public Affairs Director of KVOS-TV), is presenting Sharon Drysdale with her prize for winning an on-air contest. Both of these images are from 1958. At left, Jones is delivering an address at the launching of MSC-270, a coastal minesweeper. (Above, courtesy of the Whatcom Museum; left, courtesy of Biery [Galen] Papers and Photographs, Western Libraries Heritage Resources, Western Washington University.)

"With the introduction of a broadcast station here in Wenatchee, we shall now be able to tell the world all about the Apple Capital Of America." As reported by the *Daily World* newspaper, this is what Fred Crollard (president of the chamber of commerce) said on December 28, 1929, when KPQ went live. As the photograph shows, the antenna was located on the rooftop. KPQ was sold to Jim Wallace Sr. in 1945, and then to Cherry Creek Media in 2006, which moved the studios to the current location on Wenatchee Avenue. The original 1950s neon sign was fully restored and is a landmark on that street. (Right, courtesy of *Wenatchee World* newspaper; below, courtesy of Darlene Spargo.)

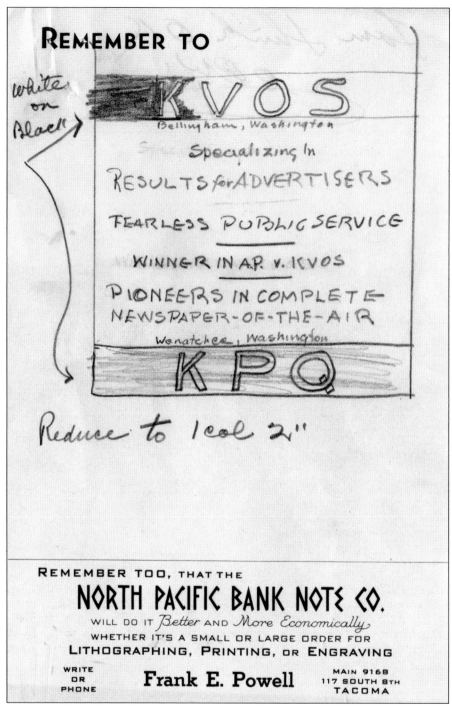

On December 14, 1936, when Rogan Jones heard about the US Supreme Court's decision in *KVOS v. Associated Press*, he set about publicizing it as a victory for his radio stations. This is his sketch of an advertisement he considered running in *Broadcasting* magazine. There is, however, no evidence that the advertisement was ever published. (Courtesy of the Center for Pacific Northwest Studies, Western Libraries Heritage Resources, Western Washington University.)

LAWYERS

FIRST NATIONAL BANK BUILDING

WENATCHEE, WASHINGTON

Oct. 25, 1929.

Prof. E. S. Meany,
4024-9th Ave. N. E.,
Seattle, Wash.

Dear Professor Meany:

I just learned that you met with a serious accident some little time ago but that you are getting along very nicely and will soon be around again among the boys and girls whom you love so well at the University.

I just dropped Mr. Condon a note telling him that I was going to make a supreme effort to be over at the homecoming on November 9th and if so, I shall certainly take time to run down to see you.

Just to make you feel that Wenatchee has not forgotten you, I am going to send by parcel post a box of Wenatchee's famous Extra Fancy Delicious that you and Mrs. Meany can enjoy. While these will taste fairly well now, I think they will be a little better in about ten days or two weeks or even around Thanksgiving time.

I sincerely trust that you will get along nicely and that you will soon be up and around again as usual.

Very sincerely yours,

Fred M. Crollard

FMC.J

When it opened, the Cascadian featured a "Wenatchee Apple Shop" in the foyer. It offered the shipping of boxes of apples across the country. Fred Crollard is an example of a prominent Wenatcheeite who took advantage of such a service when he mailed apples to a University of Washington professor. (Courtesy of the University of Washington Libraries, Special Collections, Edmond S. Meany papers, box 55, folder 7.)

The "Wenatchee Apple Shop" was run by Pearl Luce, wife of W. Foster Luce, of the Interstate Fruit Growers Company, which produced apple box labels such as the one pictured here. Upon entering the store, guests and customers were greeted by a series of pristine refrigerated cases, heaving with fruit. Beyond varieties of apples, one could choose from a selection of pears, peaches, apricots, cherries, plums, and other seasonal fruits from orchards across the Wenatchee Valley. Locally produced cider was also available for purchase. In the 1950s, the hotel introduced a new way of buying apples: vending machines. (Left, courtesy of *Wenatchee World*; below, courtesy of the Special Collections, University of California, Davis Library, Box 25, Lug Label Collection.)

The Cascadian's Apple Shop also sold Aplets candies. Still proudly handmade today in the small Liberty Orchards factory in Cashmere (12 miles to the northwest of Wenatchee), and principally known by the brand names Aplets & Cotlets, these fruit-flavored, Turkish Delight–style candies first appeared in late 1919–early 1920. Consequently, the opening of the Cascadian provided the company with a valuable opportunity to market its new product, and in collaboration with the hotel, a unique advertising strategy was born. Any guest who stayed at the Cascadian found a small container, inside of which was a piece of the candy, waiting for them in their room. A card told guests the story of this local "confection of the fairies" and encouraged them to stop by the hotel's Apple Shop to purchase some. (Both, courtesy of Liberty Orchards.)

"Cascadian" Hotel, Wenatchee, Wash.

Renowned photographer Arthur G. Simmer took this Wenatchee Avenue view of the Cascadian Hotel in the early 1930s. A native of Germany, Simmer arrived in Wenatchee with his family in 1921, setting up a photography studio. From then until 1939, he took thousands of photographs capturing the life of Wenatchee and its citizens. (Courtesy of WVMCC.)

Three

ELSIE PARRISH V. WEST COAST HOTEL COMPANY

Elsie Parrish was employed as a chambermaid at the Cascadian Hotel from August 1933 until May 1935. She was fortunate to find a job during the Great Depression, and she worked full-time, trying to put food on the table for herself and her family. However, she was paid far less than she was legally entitled to because the hotel refused to comply with the terms of the 1913 Washington law that set minimum wages for women working in that State. Elsie decided to take the hotel to court in order to try and get the $216.19 in back pay that she was owed. This was a very brave decision because the Cascadian was such a prominent employer in town. In court, C.B. Conner, a Wenatchee lawyer who decided to take her case pro bono, represented Elsie. The lawsuit went all the way up to the US Supreme Court.

The West Coast Hotel Company—the Cascadian's operating company—claimed that the state law violated its constitutional right to hire a woman for any amount of money that she was willing to work for. At this point in American legal history, this legal argument was consistent with previous Supreme Court rulings, and no one expected Elsie to win. The justices in Washington, DC, heard oral arguments in *West Coast Hotel Company v. Elsie Parrish* in December 1936 and issued their final ruling in the case on March 29, 1937. Reversing one of their previous decisions, a slim majority decided the case in Elsie's favor, concluding that governments could enact such "protective" laws because women workers were particularly vulnerable to exploitation by "unscrupulous employers."

This landmark decision prompted hundreds of women, all across Washington State, to take their employers to court in order to try and get the back pay they were entitled to. The decision paved the way for countless national and state laws that vastly improved conditions for the nation's workers (both men and women), including establishing minimum wages and maximum hours of employment.

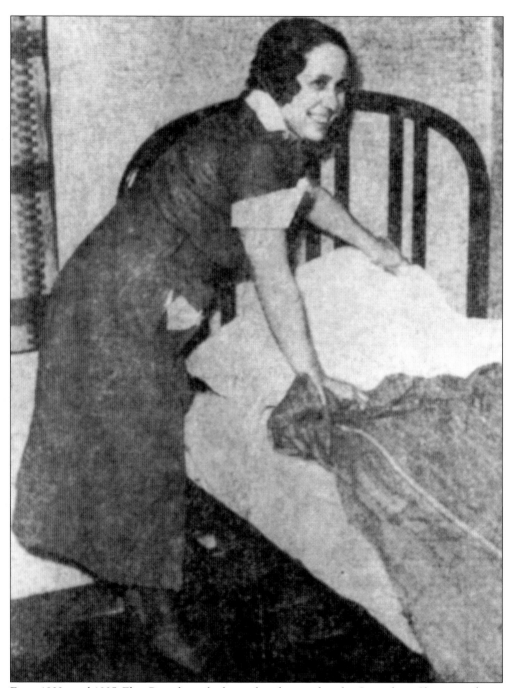

From 1933 until 1935, Elsie Parrish worked as a chambermaid at the Cascadian. She stepped into history when she sued the hotel for the difference between what she was paid and the $14.50 per 48-hour week, or 30¢ an hour, established as a minimum wage for women in Washington State. She is pictured making a bed at the Jim Hill Hotel in Omak, Washington, in November 1936. (Courtesy of WVMCC.)

Sen. George U. Piper (pictured here on the far left of the bottom row of this lineup of members of the Washington State Senate in 1913) introduced the bill that became the 1913 Washington minimum-wages-for-women law. It was the first bill of its kind to be brought up for debate during this session of the state legislature. (Courtesy of the Washington State Archives.)

Ernest Lister was the Democratic governor of Washington from 1913 to 1919. In his inauguration speech on January 15, 1913, he gave the legislature some advice: "Follow public opinion rather than . . . rush in advance of it." When Lister signed the minimum-wages-for-women bill into law in March, he believed he was following his own advice because of widespread support for this type of reform. (Courtesy of the Portraits of State Governors, 1889–2004, Washington State Archives, Digital Archives.)

When the US Supreme Court struck down a minimum-wages-for-women law in 1923, cartoonist Rollin Kirby satirized the decision. His cartoon, which ran in the *New York World* newspaper, bore the following, instantly famous caption: "This decision affirms your constitutional right to starve." This became a rallying cry for many labor activists, including the National Consumers' League, as this image shows. (Courtesy of the Library of Congress.)

In 1905, the US Supreme Court decided that the 1897 New York Bakeshop Act was unconstitutional because it violated freedom of contract. Joseph Lochner, who ran a small family bakery on South Street in Utica, New York, challenged the law. Proponents of the law had contended that it was a legally valid way of addressing the health concerns faced by bakers working long hours. The legal precedent set in *Lochner v. New York* stood as a major obstacle in the path of progressive reformers who wanted to enact other labor laws. The bakery is pictured here in an early-20th-century advertisement (right) and a 1947 photograph. (Both, courtesy of the Oneida County History Center.)

Joseph F. Lochner

248-250 South Street   Utica, N. Y.

LOCHNER'S

is one of the oldest and most reliable

Bakeries

in Central New York

We pride ourselves on Uniformity, Purity, Cleanliness

Fred Crollard, a prominent Wenatchee attorney, was the president of the chamber of commerce in 1929 and participated in the ground-breaking ceremony for the Cascadian. He would later represent the West Coast Hotel Company in its lawsuit against former Cascadian chambermaid Elsie Parrish. (Courtesy of the Crollard family.)

At a banquet held at the Cascadian on June 21, 1963, three men received awards in recognition of their many years of civic leadership in Wenatchee. Pictured from left to right are G. Harry Whiteman (who established a successful fuel distribution company in the town), Ward Jesseph (a prominent banker, and operator of the McArthur Fruit Co. in nearby Entiat), and Fred Crollard. (Courtesy of the Crollard family.)

When Chelan County was formed in March 1899, Wenatchee and Waterville battled for the county seat. Wenatchee argued that the intercontinental railroad made it the obvious choice. The question was settled when the Wenatchee Development Co. donated a vacant building, built in 1901, to the city for a courthouse. The present courthouse, designed by prominent local architect Ludwig Solberg, was erected in 1924. (Courtesy of HJK.)

This picture of US Supreme Court Justice Owen Roberts relaxing at his summer home in Kimberton, Pennsylvania, in August 1936, was featured in the article about *West Coast Hotel v. Parrish* that appeared in the April 1937 edition of *Life* magazine. Justice Roberts cast the key vote to uphold the Washington State minimum wages law for women in the *Parrish* case.

CHARLES E. HUGHES
Republican Candidate for President
Rotogravured by the Water Color Company, New York.

Charles Evans Hughes became chief justice of the US Supreme Court in 1930. He wrote the majority opinion in *West Coast Hotel v. Parrish*. He was previously a member of the court but resigned his associate justiceship in 1916 in order to run for (and very nearly win) the presidency (he is seen here in his campaign photograph). Consequently, he did not participate in the reconsideration of a 1917 case involving Oregon's minimum wage law. However, during the first round of oral arguments in that case in December 1914, Hughes had seemed inclined to uphold that law. In *Parrish*, he made good on that inclination. When he announced that decision, he did so with what historian William E. Leuchtenburg described as bouts of linguistic "eloquence, even passion" that "few thought him capable of."

Although the Cascadian finally closed as a hotel in the 1970s, some of the original equipment still remains in the basement of the building. One example is this American Aircraft–brand dryer built by the American Laundry Machinery Company. It is the type of laundry machine that Elsie Parrish would have used during her time as a chambermaid in the 1930s. (Courtesy of HJK.)

Pictured is an example of the Cascadian Hotel's stationery. Elsie Parrish was employed as a chambermaid at the Cascadian at the time this letter was mailed. The Pacific Telephone and Telegraph Company, to whom this letter (sender unknown) was sent, was founded in 1906. Its name did not change from the 1910s until the 1980s. Today, it is Pacific Bell. (Courtesy of HJK.)

Elsie's first marriage was to Roy Lee in 1915; her maiden name was Murray. She was 15 years old, and he was 24. They were married somewhere between Kansas and Montana, during the period of time when they relocated from Bell Township, Kansas, to the Murray homestead in Coffee Creek, Montana. Elsie divorced Roy early in the 1930s. (Courtesy of the Murray family.)

Ernest and Elsie Parrish got married in Wenatchee on July 28, 1934, after Elsie worked her day's shift at the Cascadian. Ernest was Elsie's second husband. At one point, Ernest was a traveling meat salesman, and Wenatchee was the midway point on his route. However, city directories from the early 1930s also indicate he resided in Wenatchee for a period of time before marrying Elsie. (Courtesy of WVMCC.)

These two photographs of Omak, Washington, were taken in the mid-1930s. In 1936, Elsie and Ernie Parrish decided to relocate to this town, population 2,500, which is nestled in the North Central region of the state, 45 miles south of the Canadian border. Omak is situated 100 miles north of Wenatchee. After Elsie initiated her lawsuit against the Cascadian, it was difficult for the couple to find work in Wenatchee. They were attracted to Omak by job opportunities at the Biles-Coleman sawmill, and this was a chance for Ernest to return to his native Okanogan Highlands. Elsie found employment cleaning rooms at the Jim Hill Hotel. (Both, courtesy of MASC-WSU.)

When the Parrishes moved from Wenatchee to Omak in early 1936, Ernie found work at the Biles-Coleman sawmill. Job opportunities arose there when non-union workers were brought in to replace those who went out on strike in May 1936 and did not return until August 1938. (Courtesy of MASC-WSU.)

As their great-granddaughter recalls, "things were a lot easier" for Elsie "when she married Ernie," and upon moving to California in the 1950s, Elsie no longer had to work. She was able to enjoy being a wife, mother, grandmother, and great-grandmother. However, there was never any doubt that Elsie, just as she had always done, "wore the pants in the family." It was Elsie who "did all the talking." (Courtesy of Debra Parrish Stewart.)

Debra Parrish Stewart is Elsie's great-granddaughter. She lived with Elsie and Ernie on and off from the late 1960s until Elsie's death in 1980. Debra "misses" Elsie "all the time," and she has numerous fond memories of this time in her life, including the enticing smell of Elsie's freshly baked biscuits, dripping with butter and honey, and her first job, at Carl's Jr., that Elsie got her. (Courtesy of HJK.)

Pictured here enjoying a family dinner, most likely at a local restaurant close to Elsie and Ernest Parrish's home in Anaheim, California, sometime early in the 1950s, are (from left to right) Pauline Murray (Debra Parrish Stewart's aunt), Elsie Parrish, Darald Parrish, and Ernest Parrish. (Courtesy of Debra Parrish Stewart.)

Elsie and Ernie Parrish are pictured here with their grandson Darald. Born in 1935 in what is today called Moses Lake, in central Washington State, Darald was the son of Elsie's eldest daughter Vera, and her husband, J.D. Hollingsworth. Darald was Debra Parrish Stewart's father. (Courtesy of Debra Parrish Stewart.)

Elsie Parrish is pictured here with Darald. This photograph was taken in the yard of Elsie's house in southern California. Darald was stationed in California during part of his service in the United States Air Force, affording him the opportunity to spend some time with his grandparents. A Korean War veteran, Darald rose to the rank of staff sergeant. (Courtesy of Debra Parrish Stewart.)

Debra Parrish Stewart is pictured here, on the day of her graduation from junior high, with her great-grandparents Elsie and Ernie Parrish, and with Elsie and Debra's mother, Arlene. Elsie, who was like a mother to Debra, bought this graduation dress for her. Elsie raised the teenage Debra at the same time as she focused on the many pleasures of her "retirement" because Ernest brought home a regular income from his work at Knotts Berry Farm, from where Debra got her pet turtle and rabbits. Elsie made all of the clothes for Debra's dolls, and the avid gardener that she was, she would take Debra to a local nursery and surreptitiously put clippings of plants into her purse, saying that this ultimately was very good for the shrubs. (Both, courtesy of Debra Parrish Stewart.)

Pictured here at a family gathering are, from left to right, Mildred Malanska (the mother of Arlene [Malanska] Parrish), her son-in-law Darald Parrish, Arlene (Darald's wife), and Elsie Parrish. Arlene and Darald got married in January 1956. Their daughter Debra was born in December 1956. (Courtesy of Debra Parrish Stewart.)

In 1991, Barbara K. Roberts was sworn in as Oregon's 34th, but first female, governor. Barbara's mother, Carmen, was born in Big Sandy, Montana, in 1917. Elsie Parrish was her aunt. Roberts trail-blazed her way into history, especially regarding women's rights. Not until 2017, when contacted by one of the authors of this volume, was she aware that her great-aunt had also made history. (Courtesy of Edmund Keene.)

Four

FAMOUS GUESTS

Throughout its history, the Cascadian Hotel used advertising strategies to try and attract guests, both famous and humble. The hotel had only been open for two years when it hosted Clyde Pangborn and Hugh Herndon Jr. When the two daredevil pilots failed in their attempt to fly around the world, they decided to compete for a $50,000 prize offered by Japan's *Asahi Shimbun* newspaper for the first nonstop flight across the Pacific. After a harrowing flight and near-death plunge over the Pacific Ocean, the *Miss Veedol* arrived over Wenatchee (Pangborn was born in nearby Bridgeport). At 7:14 a.m. on October 5, 1931, Pangborn cut off the fuel and ignition switches and set the plane down in a cloud of dust. The news of their achievement went around the world, and the Cascadian rolled out the red carpet.

Prior to taking off from Misawa, a young boy handed five apples to Pangborn, reminding him of Wenatchee's apples. Pangborn subsequently arranged for Wenatchee's mayor to send five cuttings of Richard Delicious apples to Misawa. Their cuttings and seedlings were distributed throughout Japan and are still grown there today.

In May 1933, Ernestine Schumann-Heink, a world-renowned opera star, stayed at the Cascadian when she was on a concert tour of the West Coast. Her first professional appearance, in 1878, as a 17-year-old, came in Verdi's *Il Trovatore* in Dresden, Germany. She later became an American citizen, entertaining troops and raising money for wounded soldiers during World War I. Schumann-Heink had a weekly radio show. She sang *Silent Night* on the radio in 1926, and it became a tradition that lasted through 1935.

Nat King Cole was 20 years old when he formed the King Cole Trio. He earned 58 gold record awards and gave a command performance for Queen Elizabeth II. However, he had to battle racism his entire career. He is credited with breaking the color barrier in Wenatchee in 1947. After the King Cole Trio played a concert in town, the Cascadian initially refused them rooms for the night. That changed after Cole placed a call to Eddie Carlson, vice president of Western Hotels.

In their book about main street hotels, John Jakle and Keith Sculle's description of the typical layout of a railroad boomtown applies to Wenatchee: the "Main Street . . . paralleled the tracks . . . or crossed the tracks on the perpendicular. Most railroad-era hotels were located in business districts close to" those tracks. However, in Wenatchee, something additional parallels those

tracks: the mighty Columbia River. This photograph looks northwest towards the confluence of the Columbia and the Wenatchee River. Popular among visitors and residents is the Apple Capital Loop Trail, a 10-mile recreational walking, running, and cycling path that opened in 1994. The trail follows the river on both sides, connected by two bridges. (Courtesy of HJK.)

CASCADIAN HOTEL
WENATCHEE, WASHINGTON

Howard Presar was just 22 years old when he arrived in Wenatchee and wrote this postcard to his sister Florence Presar Ruck back home in Ohio. His salary of $16 a week was below the median income for single men in 1946 of $21 a week, so he probably needed to work two jobs; hence the restaurant position. Hopefully, he received his share of tips. Howard returned to Ohio before 1950, married, and fathered three daughters. He owned a string of laundromats and Howie's Carpet Cleaning Service. In his youth, Howard played the violin while his father called square dances. As a young man, he joined the George Bundy Band and played guitar throughout northwest Ohio. Howard died in Ohio in 2008 at the age of 84. (Both, courtesy of HJK.)

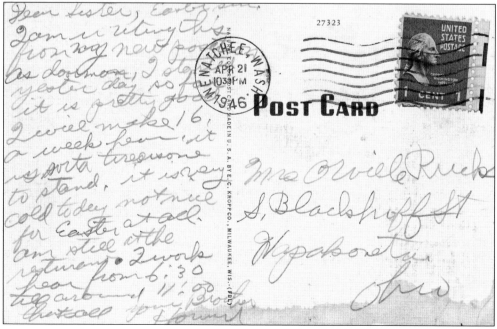

This exterior view of the Cascadian Hotel, from 1944, shows the sides facing Wenatchee Avenue and First Street. The sign on the left front corner of the building reads, "For a Fresh Start Stop at a Hotel," and features a saluting bellboy. The Coffee Shop is advertised on the far right of the sign. (Courtesy of WVMCC.)

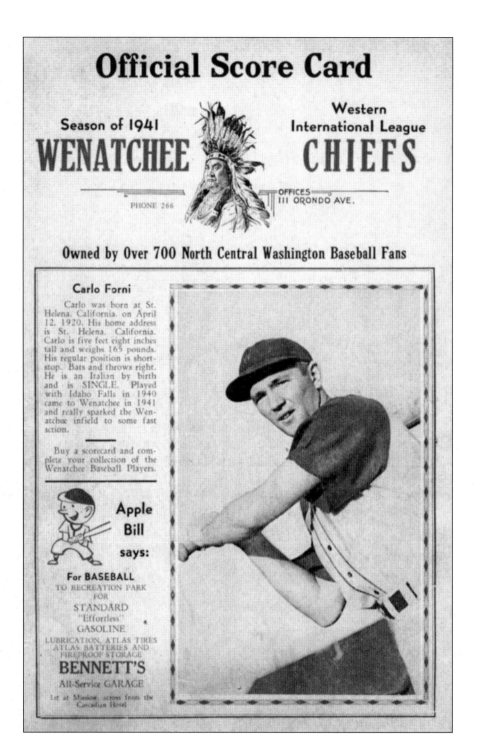

Official Score Card

Season of 1941

WENATCHEE

Western
International League

CHIEFS

PHONE 266

OFFICES
111 ORONDO AVE.

Owned by Over 700 North Central Washington Baseball Fans

Carlo Forni

Carlo was born at St. Helena, California, on April 12, 1920. His home address is St. Helena, California. Carlo is five feet eight inches tall and weighs 165 pounds. His regular position is shortstop. Bats and throws right. He is an Italian by birth and is SINGLE. Played with Idaho Falls in 1940 came to Wenatchee in 1941 and really sparked the Wenatchee infield to some fast action.

Buy a scorecard and complete your collection of the Wenatchee Baseball Players.

Apple
Bill
says:

For BASEBALL
TO RECREATION PARK
FOR
STANDARD
"Effortless"
GASOLINE
LUBRICATION, ATLAS TIRES
ATLAS BATTERIES AND
FIREPROOF STORAGE

BENNETT'S

All-Service GARAGE

1st at Mission, across from the
Cascadian Hotel

Oftentimes, the Cascadian benefited from indirect advertising, as is shown here on the cover of this 1941 Wenatchee Chiefs baseball scorecard. (The Chiefs were a minor league team that existed from 1937–1965). The scorecard features advertising sponsorship provided by Bennett's Garage, which was built at the same time as the Cascadian (half a block from the hotel) with the intention that the hotel's guests would use it. (Courtesy of the David Eskenazi Collection.)

As soon as it opened, the Cascadian Hotel was the kind of place where prominent visitors stayed and dined. During its first year of operation, one such visitor was William Wallace Atterbury. A career employee of the Pennsylvania Railroad, by the time he dined at the Cascadian Atterbury had risen to become the company's president (he held that position from 1925 to 1935). (Courtesy of the Hagley Library, Image AVD_1994309_01_01_001.)

Pangborn – Herndon, Trans-Pacific Fliers, arriving at Wenatchee, Oct. 5, 1931.

Clyde Pangborn and Hugh Herndon Jr. pose with their plane, the *Miss Veedol*, after their historic nonstop trans-Pacific flight. The pair took off from Sabashiro Beach, Japan, on October 3, 1931. They headed for Seattle, Washington, 5,500 miles away. Although not the original landing site, Wenatchee's Fancher Field proved an adequate substitute after weather conditions prevented the pair from landing in either Seattle or Spokane. (Courtesy of WVMCC.)

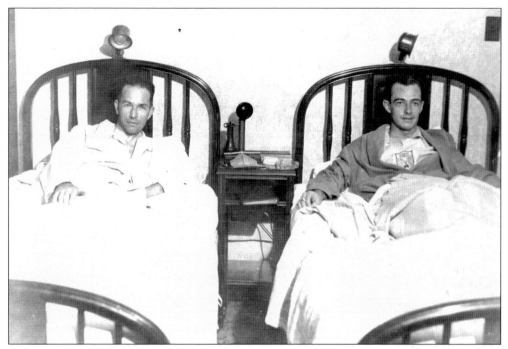

Upon completing their historic flight, Clyde Pangborn and Hugh Herndon Jr. received congratulations from around the globe. The *Wenatchee Daily World* newspaper reporter Carl M. Cleveland's headline was relayed to the worldwide wire services: "Pangborn-Herndon span pacific . . . boy are we glad to get here: Pangborn puts it . . . it's like a dream come true." Wenatchee gave the two men a multifaceted heroes' welcome. For example, the Kiwanis Club lined up in front of the Cascadian to honor the two men following a noon luncheon. What the two men really wanted, however, was rest. The hotel provided them with this, but photographers were nevertheless eager to record every aspect of their comings and goings; hence the publication of numerous photographs, from various angles, of Clyde and Hugh simply laying in their beds in their room at the Cascadian. (Both, courtesy of WVMCC.)

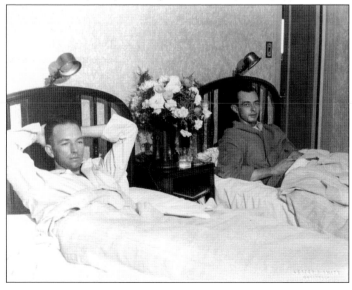

Hugh Herndon Jr. and Clyde Pangborn enjoyed breakfast in their room at the Cascadian Hotel. Both men autographed this photograph to state patrolman Jack Columbus, "the first man to greet us landing in Wenatchee." Pangborn's mother was adamant that her son would ultimately choose Wenatchee as his landing site. She was among 30 people who waited through the night for the fliers to arrive. (Courtesy of WVMCC.)

By the 1940s, the Thrifty Drug store had replaced Pay Less Drugs in the Olympia Hotel Building. Visible in front of the store is the Pangborn Clock. This clock was built in 1915 and purchased in 1920 by Percy Pangborn to sit in front of his jewelry store. Percy was the older brother of the famous aviator Clyde Pangborn. The clock now graces Wenatchee's Centennial Park. (Courtesy of HJK.)

Inscribed with the words "Three Big Shots," this photograph features Clyde Pangborn (left) and Hugh Herndon Jr. (right) posing with Ray W. Clark, the manager of the Cascadian Hotel. Clark was an enthusiastic booster of the region and became treasurer of the development group promoting the Grand Coulee Dam. Everyone wanted to congratulate the two fliers. Pictured from left to right at breakfast at the Cascadian: Hugh Herndon Jr.; John A. Gellatly, lieutenant governor of Washington; Clyde Pangborn; and Ray Clark. Gellatly was known by the title "Wenatchee First Citizen." He held every local office and twice ran for governor. The photograph has autographs from both fliers to Clark. (Both, courtesy of WVMCC.)

Madame Ernestine Schumann-Heink, an internationally known German-Bohemian American contralto, toured Wenatchee in May 1933. She no longer had the stunning voice to which the world of opera had first been introduced in 1878, but could still captivate audiences. While performing at the Liberty Theater, she stayed at the Cascadian. She autographed this copy of her photograph to Muriel Taggart, the hotel employee summoned to work on the guest's nails and hair. (Courtesy of WVMCC.)

The Liberty Theater, across whose footlights Ernestine Schumann Heink talked to Wenatcheeites in 1933, was built in 1919, and still stands today. "The Show Palace" sign painted on the building's exterior brickwork remains, but much of the Liberty's external majesty has now gone. Regardless, it remains a working movie theater. It is located a stone's throw from the Cascadian building. (Courtesy of WVMCC.)

This view of Wenatchee Avenue looking north to the Cascadian was taken by renowned photographer Arthur G. Simmer in the early 1930s. The Liberty Theater is still in operation. In front of the Liberty is the Kress 5-10-25 Store. The building followed the Chicago Commercial style common among Kress stores with its Art Deco–inspired styling. Kress bragged there were 4,275 different articles on sale in 1934. (Courtesy of HJK.)

In 1947, the King Cole Trio, led by Nat King Cole, played the Wenatchee Auditorium as part of their national tour. After the show, the three men were refused rooms at the Cascadian; not until Cole placed a call to Eddie Carlson, vice president of Western Hotels, would the band members be permitted to stay at the hotel. On that night, "a color line fell in Wenatchee." (Courtesy of the New York Public Library.)

Five

A NEW MOTEL ANNEX
FOR THE 1960s

In 1961, a new Cascadian motor hotel extension was built, at a cost of over $300,000. It was "designed," as Clair Van Divort, the president of the corporation overseeing construction, proclaimed in a *Wenatchee Daily World* article, "to be at least five years ahead of the times in motor hotel construction." Operated, like the Cascadian, by Western Hotels, it was connected to the back of the original hotel structure by a covered third-floor walkway. The motel could also be accessed from First Street. It consisted of 24 units, 16 of which had private covered porches. They were built around a heated swimming pool and patio area. The units and pool were on the second and third levels of the structure; the first (street) level consisted of a parking garage that included a ski-waxing room. The facility opened to the public in October, and at the open house, visitors were treated to musical entertainment provided by the acts who were performing at the main hotel.

The following year, the Seaman Building adjoining the Cascadian on Wenatchee Avenue was converted into a 700-person-capacity banquet room, giving the hotel valuable additional conference meeting space. This reflected the rapidly increasing number of conventions attracted to Wenatchee (principally as a result of a chamber of commerce initiative called "Conventions Unlimited"). Indeed, by the end of 1962, the Cascadian had already booked 33 conventions for the following year (a year that also saw the chamber of commerce establish a new tourist information center further up North Wenatchee Avenue).

However, while the Cascadian's owners considered the motor inn an important (and economically essentially) addition, they failed to appreciate that it was built at the tail end of a decade-long boom, which, by the mid-1960s, had seen over 60,000 such motels spring up nationwide (including many in Wenatchee). Rather than being "five years ahead of the times," the new motor inn was approximately five years behind the times.

This 1950s Cascadian postcard proclaimed the hotel was "the city's finest hotel, operated by Western Hotels and providing the ultimate in service and comfort for the many visitors to the 'Apple Capital of The World.'" Each guest was greeted with a piece of Aplet candy made in Cashmere. The candy was first produced in 1919–1920 as a way to use up surplus apples. (Courtesy of HJK.)

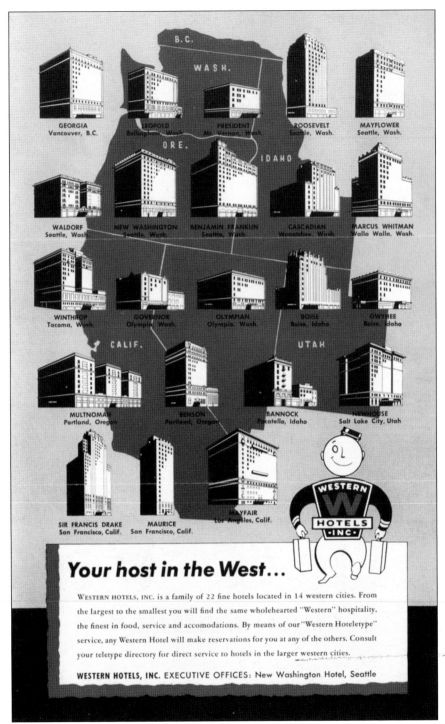

This poster, from the 1950s–1960s, is an example of the marketing and promotion materials that the Western Hotels Company posted at its properties. This one, from the Cascadian, served to inform visitors of the other Western properties that they could visit, and the ease with which reservations at such locations could be made. (Courtesy of MASC-WSU.)

Matchbooks, which were first patented in the United States in the 1890s, were particularly popular methods of publicity for various different businesses in the 1940s, 1950s, and 1960s. These matchbook covers (inside and out) advertise numerous aspects of the Cascadian Hotel's services and features. Three companies produced the selection pictured here. The Diamond Match Company (which had been in existence since the Civil War), the Universal Match Corporation (with manufacturing locations in Seattle and St. Louis), and the Maryland Match Company (Seattle). The outside covers all feature apples in their designs. As this selection also shows, it was common for the insides of the Cascadian's matchbook covers to list other Western Hotels properties. (Both, courtesy of HJK.)

In the 1950s–1960s, as part of its external marketing campaign, the Western Hotels Company created a promotional "three dollar bill," which recipients could use as partial payment for overnight stays at various properties. This bill could be redeemed for a weekend stay at one of six different properties in Washington and Montana. In addition to the Cascadian, it could be used at the Davenport (Spokane), the Finlen (Butte), the Marcus Whitman (Walla Walla), the Northern (Billings), and the Rainbow (Great Falls). The bills also served as a form of advertising for the Western "Hoteltype" service; the staff at any Western hotel would make free reservations at any other Western Hotel for their guests. (Both, courtesy of MASC-WSU.)

When the Cascadian first opened, it only served food and drinks in the coffee shop. This photograph, from 1945, shows the Apple Box Room bar and lounge that was added to the hotel. Reflecting the layout of the hotel's early communal areas, this gathering space featured several types and styles of seating designed to cater to guests' different needs and desires. (Courtesy of WVMCC.)

In the 1950s, the famed Apple Box restaurant became a prominent element of the Cascadian and was featured in much of the hotel's advertising. An apple tree stood in the center of the room, and the walls were lined with labels from apple boxes; hence the restaurant's name. This photograph is from 1957. (Courtesy of MASC-WSU.)

FROM THE APPLEBOX
CASCADIAN HOTEL & MOTOR INN
WENATCHEE, WASHINGTON

COCKTAILS

ALEXANDERS 90
  Brandy, Creme de Cacao, Cream

BACARDI 90
  Rum, Lime Juice, Grenadine

DAIQUIRI 90
  Rum, Lime Juice and Sugar

GIBSON 80
  Gin or Vodka, Vermouth

GIMLET 90
  Gin, Rose's Lime Juice, Sugar

GRASSHOPPER 90
  Cream de Menthe, Creme de Cacao, Cream

MANHATTAN 80
  Whiskey, Sweet Vermouth, Bitters

MARTINI 80
  Gin or Vodka, Dry Vermouth

ORANGE BLOSSOM 90
  Gin, Orange Juice, Sugar

OLD FASHIONED 80
  Whiskey, Sugar and Bitters

PINK LADY 90
  Gin, Cream, Lemon and Grenadine

SIDE CAR 95
  Brandy, Cointreau, Lime Juice

STINGER 90
  Brand and Creme de Menthe

DRINK LIST

LIQUORS

BAR BOURBON	.70
STRAIGHT WHISKIES . .	.80
BONDED WHISKIES . . .	.85
SCOTCH	.85 & 1.00
CANADIAN WHISKIES . .	.80
IRISH WHISKIES . . .	.80
BAR BRANDY	.80
COGNAC	.95
VODKA	.70
GIN	.70 & .95
RUMS	.75 & .85

MEDIUM

FIZZES, Plain	.80
GIN AND TONIC . . .	.75
MOSCOW MULE . . .	.75
SCREWDRIVER . . .	.75
SOURS	.75
RICKEYS	.75

TAME

LEMON OR LIMEADE . .	.30
7-UP, PEPSI, GINGER ALE	.30
GINGER BEER — LIME .	.40

TALL

COLLINS	.75
CUBA LIBRE	.75
SINGAPORE SLING . . .	1.25
MILK PUNCHES	90
EGGNOGS	.95
SILVER, GOLDEN, ROYAL OR NEW ORLEANS FIZZES	.95

CORDIALS

B AND B	.95
BENEDICTINE	.95
COINTREAU	.95
CHERRY HEERING . . .	.95
CREME DE MENTHE FRAPPE	.95
DRAMBUIE	.95
GALLIANO	1.00
KAHLUA	.95
KING ALPHONSE . . .	1.00
OTHER CORDIALS . . .	.80

OTHER

BEER	.35 & .40
WINE . . . CHAMPAGNE	

ALL PRICES INCLUDE 4% WASHINGTON STATE SALES TAX
CABARET TAX WILL BE CHARGED DURING ENTERTAINMENT

Drink prices have certainly changed since those listed on this 1960 drink list from the Apple Box Restaurant in the Cascadian. Soft drinks were listed under "Tame," and listed under "Other" were beer and champagne. Pepsi was 30¢ and beer 35¢. A cabaret tax was charged during entertainment. (Courtesy of Dian [Ulrich] Thompson estate.)

On February 17, 1961, the *Wenatchee Daily World* newspaper ran an article under the following headline: "Plans Announced for Deluxe Downtown Motel." This photograph, which appeared in the newspaper, shows the presentation, to the public, of an artist's rendering of the planned addition to the hotel. Clair Van Divort is on the left, and Robert Dupar is on the right. (Courtesy of MASC-WSU.)

Postwar America was the apex of automobile tourism in America, and postcards were the perfect advertisement. "Motels" was a name coined by Arthur Heineman, the owner of the Milestone Mo-Tel (an abbreviation of "motor hotel") in San Luis Obispo, California. They offered convenience, ample parking, clean, modern rooms, and the latest in amenities such as TVs and air conditioning. Competition was high, with 61,000 motels dotting the map in 1960. On postcards, like these of Scotty's Motel and the American MoteLodge, they were shown under idealized settings with their swimming pools tempting tourists. Postcards served as a means of communication, a travel souvenir, or a way for vacationers to document their journey or add to a personal collection. For motels, postcards were a primary means of advertising. (Both, courtesy of HJK.)

Motels were built with convenience in mind. They were close to the highway, with easy access, and provided ample parking at the door. The pre–World War II auto cabins gave way to the more efficient I-, L-, or U-shaped layout that included guest rooms, an attached manager's office, a small reception, and in some cases, a small diner and a swimming pool. The rooms opened directly on to the parking lot for ease in unloading suitcases. If a second story was added, open stairwells and balconies accessed it. Architectural design was simple and utilitarian. Bathroom plumbing was stacked together, and each room had individual heating and cooling units. Room design was standardized so that travelers knew what to expect. For added convenience, a motel might offer several units with kitchenettes and on-site laundry facilities. (Both, courtesy of HJK.)

During its prime in the 1960s and 1970s, the Chieftain Motel was a premier motel with a five-star restaurant and the Pow Wow Room lounge. The unusual night view of the Chieftain with its flaming torch and the couple exiting from the fashionable Ford Thunderbird sets the scene for a romantic night out. The exceptional restaurant was uncommon among motels. As a nod to Wenatchee's apple capital theme, a loaf of apple bread was served with each meal. The day scene is a more typical postcard featuring the usual amenities of a pool and room phones. The motel is now part of the Best Western Corporation and was remodeled in 2008, but the restaurant no longer exists. (Both, courtesy of HJK.)

Rooney's Motor Lodge was located on North Wenatchee Avenue. The Coffee Shop was front and center and, like the Chieftain Restaurant, drew locals as well as travelers with its home cooking–style meals. It also drew travelers from the other smaller motels in the immediate area that did not have onsite cafes. (Courtesy of HJK.)

The Cascadian Motor Inn annex added in 1961 incorporated the outside entrance arrangement of rooms surrounding a pool, typical of most modern motels. When the Cascadian closed in 1971, the motel annex rooms were remodeled into 23 condominiums and renamed the Uptowner Motel. (Courtesy of HJK.)

This photograph looks southeast across North Mission Street toward the Mission Court Apartments located at the intersection of North Mission and First Streets in Wenatchee. The photograph was taken in 1961 during the building of the Cascadian motor inn annex and shows the construction of the swimming pool. (Courtesy of MASC-WSU.)

When the motor inn annex was added to the Cascadian in 1961, it was connected to the original hotel building by a sky bridge, shown here under construction. The bridge was removed in 1971 when plans for redevelopment of the motor inn were developed entirely separately from plans for the closure and repurposing of the hotel. (Courtesy of MASC-WSU.)

Six

FAMOUS EMPLOYEES

Over the years, the Cascadian Hotel provided a good place to begin one's career in hotel management. Willard E. Abel had managerial experience before coming to the Cascadian in 1934, but the Wenatchee hotel nevertheless played an important role in his career. By the mid-1960s, he was a senior vice president of Western International Hotels (WIH), overseeing the International Division. In 1965 he was named Hotelman of the Year by that company.

Gina Tucker and Harry Mullikin, who both became prominent members of the country's hospitality industry, started their careers at the Cascadian. A native Washingtonian, Georgina "Gina" Tucker (née Petheram) graduated from the State College of Washington in 1933 with a BS in Home Economics, whereupon she entered into the employment of the Cascadian as a trainee food service manager. That began her 42 years of service for WIH or one of its subsidiaries. Four years after receiving the 1971 Thurston-Dupar Inspirational Award, the company's "highest employee award distinction," she finally retired, having risen to the prestigious position of executive in charge of housekeeping of the grand Century Plaza Hotel in Los Angeles.

Harry Mullikin and his parents came to Wenatchee during the Great Depression after floods devastated their native Arkansas. The Cascadian was a source of income for Harry in the early 1940s as he worked there after school, on the weekends, and during his winter and summer breaks. Originally hired in the spring of 1942, he was primarily an elevator operator, but he also performed bellman, busboy, porter, night janitor, room clerk, and houseman duties, eventually working 10-hour shifts as he and the other young men of Wenatchee filled the holes in the town's workforce left by World War II enlistments. Living and working in Spokane and then Seattle after graduating from Washington State College in 1949 (where he studied hotel management), Mullikin held various different hotel positions over the next decade. In 1973, he became president of WIH and led it through a period of unprecedented growth, resulting in a 1977 *New York Times* profile entitled "The Man Behind the Megahotels."

Family lore has it that Frank Dupar arrived in Seattle broke in the early 1900s because a thief got to his money while he was hitching a ride in a boxcar. In 1930, a successful Dupar was in a diner in Yakima, Washington, when he and Severt W. Thurston met and decided to merge their hotels. Peter and Adolph Schmidt joined them, creating Western Hotels, with Dupar becoming secretary-treasurer. (Courtesy of MASC-WSU.)

Severt W. Thurston arrived in Seattle in 1903 to pursue a vaudeville career but left show business after a human pyramid accident. A subsequent job as a hotel porter led to his forming the Maltby-Thurston hotel corporation in 1910 with Hal Maltby. In 1930, a chance meeting with Frank Dupar led to the formation of Western Hotels, of which Thurston became the first president. (Courtesy of MASC-WSU.)

Idea Party

CASCADIAN WESTERN HOTEL
DECEMBER 9, 1959

Western Hotels prided itself on service to the community. This booklet was distributed at a festive Idea Party held on December 9, 1959. Georgina Tucker, Western's assistant food director from Seattle (who got her start in hospitality in 1933 at the Cascadian), acted as hostess. The party was open to club representatives at 2:00 p.m. and the public at 7:00 p.m. Thomas Dupar welcomed attendees. Holiday-themed displays showcased decorating and menu ideas. Weddings and children's parties were also featured. Tea was served with pastries and samples of wedding cake. During a discussion period, Tucker shared 26 fundraising ideas for clubs. Attendees were encouraged to visit newly refurbished rooms located on the eighth and tenth floors. (Both, courtesy of Dian [Ulrich] Thompson estate.)

All of the Idea Party displays will be open to the general public from 7:00 P.M. to 9:00 P.M., Wednesday evening . . . No reservations or tickets required. Dinner available in the COFFEE SHOP or DINING ROOM.

— ☆ —

YOU ARE CORDIALLY INVITED
to visit the Eighth and the Tenth Floors for an informal showing of newly refinished rooms, part of a comprehensive program of renovation planned for Wenatchee's center of community entertaining and hospitality.

SUGGESTIONS FOR POSSIBLE FUND RAISING PROJECTS:

Combined with an Entertainment Feature

1. Supper Fashion Dances
2. Breakfast Parties
3. Fashion Luncheon or Tea — Hat Shows
4. Garden Tour concluded with tea at Hotel
5. Christmas House Tour concluded with Tea at Hotel
6. Spice and Herb Show
7. Specialty Parties with dishes native to a country. Hawaiian, Swedish, Argentine, Mexico, Left Bank Party.
8. Treasure Sale and Luncheon
9. Bridge Lessons in a.m., Luncheon, Bridge Party
10. Christmas Eve Luncheon, Carolers, Santa, etc.
11. Christmas Ball
12. Preview of a New Car and Cocktail Party
13. Muse de Noel
14. Art Show, sell paintings — Have Tea or Cocktails

Cascadian

MODERN FIREPROOF HOTEL
WASHED AIR COOLING SYSTEM

Wenatchee
WASHINGTON

DEAR FRIEND:

THE COLLEGE GIRLS AT THE CASCADIAN HOTEL ARE ALREADY PLANNING AN UNUSUAL THANKSGIVING DINNER. WE WISH TO ASSUME YOUR RESPONSIBILITIES OF PREPARATION AND SERVICE FOR YOUR THANKSGIVING DINNER. THE FASTIDIOUS HOSTESS WILL APPRECIATE THE DELICACIES AND APPOINTMENTS.

THESE ARE OUR SUGGESTIONS:--

FRESH PINEAPPLE, CRAB, OR SHRIMP COCKTAIL
+++++
OYSTER SOUP OR CONSOMME
+++++
CRANBERRY FRAPPE   ICED CELERY HEARTS
+++++++
ROAST TURKEY-- GIBLET GRAVY---DRESSING

TENDERLOIN STEAK--GOOSEBERRY JAM

ROAST DUCK--DRESSING--RED PEPPER JAM

WHIPPED POTATOES   WALNUT SWEET POTATOES
GLAZED ONIONS   BUTTERED PEAS
PETITE FRENCH ROLLS
+++++
GRAPEFRUIT AND POMEGRANATE SALAD
PAPRIKA WAFERS

HOT MINCE, PUMPKIN OR APPLE PIE
PLUM PUDDING WITH HARD SAUCE
CHOCOLATE SUNDAE, SHERBET
BEVERAGE
NUTS   CLUSTER RAISINS   MINTS

WE ARE OFFERING THIS DINNER FOR $1.00 IN THE DINING ROOM OR COFFEE SHOP AND $1.25 IN PRIVATE ROOMS.

SINCERELY,

Martha Meyers
Laura Frederick   *Ruth Alden*
Virginia Houtchen   *Georgina Petheram*
Helen Briggs
Edna Pryor
(Janet Smith & Betty Schiffer)

In 1933, eight recent home economics graduates from regional colleges participated in the Cascadian's hospitality training program, supervised by manager Ray Clark and his wife, Kathryn (who was in charge of housekeeping). They were in charge of planning special dining programs, such as the annual Thanksgiving dinner. This is the 1933 menu they compiled for that dinner. (Courtesy of MASC-WSU.)

Gina Tucker was one of the eight recent college graduates who arrived at the Cascadian in 1933. She trained to become a hospitality manager. She spent four decades working for Western Hotels, rising to the prestigious position of executive in charge of housekeeping of the grand Century Plaza Hotel in Los Angeles. She received the 1971 Thurston-Dupar Inspirational Award, the company's highest award, and was affectionately known as the "first lady" of the company. (Courtesy of MASC-WSU.)

As Edward E. Carlson recalls in his memoir, *Recollections of a Lucky Fellow*, Willard E. Abel was a "tall, debonair" man who was "strong on financing, tax structures, and insurance requirements." Abel came to the Cascadian in the early 1930s after holding managerial positions at the Donnelly Hotel in Yakima, Washington, and the Lewis and Clark Hotel in Mandan, North Dakota. When Ray Clark left the Cascadian in 1934, Abel became its full-time manager, and it was he who terminated Elsie Parrish's employment in May 1935. Abel's tenure at the Cascadian was interrupted by military service during World War II, but he returned to his original position there in 1945. As Carlson also notes, Abel was a "longtime protégé of Frank Dupar," and he rose to become a senior vice president of Western International Hotels. In 1965, the company named Abel as Hotelman of the Year. (Both, courtesy of MASC-WSU.)

Harry Mullikin began working at the Cascadian in 1942; he was an elevator operator, bellman, busboy, porter, night janitor, room clerk, and houseman. During his distinguished career, Mullikin spent little time out of the employment of the Western Hotels Company. In 1973, he became president of the company (now Western International Hotels). When profiled by the *New York Times* in 1977, he was described as "The Man Behind the Megahotels." (Courtesy of MASC-WSU.)

The first issue of the *Apple Worm* appeared on March 5, 1960. Edited by Billie Box, this newsletter consisted of several pages of Cascadian news, insider gossip, jokes, and notices of new hires and promotions. An article on page 2, under the column "Between the Sheets," noted the passing of Tommy Gore, a permanent resident of 24 years. (Courtesy of Dian [Ulrich] Thompson estate.)

WESTERN UNION
TELEGRAM
W. P. MARSHALL, PRESIDENT

1201

The filing time shown in the date line on domestic telegrams is STANDARD TIME at point of origin. Time of receipt is STANDARD TIME at point of destination

PRA005 SSB042

1959 DEC 2 AM 6 51

PR SEA250 NL PD=FAX SEATTLE WASH 1 =

MISS DIANE ULRICH, "MISS WESTERN" =

    CARE TOM DUPAR MANAGER CASCADIAN HOTEL WENATCHEE WASH

CONGRATULATIONS ON BEING SELECTED AS "MISS WESTERN"
YOUR WINNING SMILE REFLECTS THE CHARM AND PLEASING
PERSONALITY SO NECESSARY IN OUR PARTICULAR FIELD. SUCH
SPIRIT, WE BELIEVE CAN VERY WELL MAKE THE DIFFERENCE
BETWEEN WESTERN HOTELS AND OUR COMPETITION. MAY I EXTEND
TO YOU OUR HEARTIEST BEST WISHES ON BEHALF OF WESTERN
HOTELS PERSONNEL AND EXECUTIVES=
    S W THURSTON PRES WESTERN HOTELS INC.

THE COMPANY WILL APPRECIATE SUGGESTIONS FROM ITS PATRONS CONCERNING ITS SERVICE

In 1959, competing as Miss Cascadian, Wenatchee's Dian Ulrich was chosen as Miss Western Hotel from a field of 36 women representing their respective hotels. As part of the competition, their physical measurements were listed alongside their photographs. S.W. Thurston, president of Western Hotels, notified Ulrich of her selection via a telegram dated December 2. Congratulating Ulrich on her victory, Washington's secretary of state Victor Meyers compared her to Wenatchee's Roman Beauty, Pippin, and Delicious apples because, in his opinion, Ulrich had "the best qualities of the aforementioned fruit." The Cascadian Hotel float, featuring Ulrich, won first prize in the 1960 Washington State Apple Blossom Parade. She also represented Western Hotels at the Seattle World's Fair in 1962. (Both, courtesy of Dian [Ulrich] Thompson estate.)

State of Washington
DEPARTMENT OF STATE
Olympia

VIC MEYERS
SECRETARY OF STATE

December 10, 1959

Miss Dian Ulrich
"Miss Western Hotels Queen"
Cascadian Hotel
Wenatchee, Washington

Dear Miss Ulrich:

    For many, many years I have firmly been convinced the apples of the Wenatchee valley were as sweet as any found anywhere. It is now a further education to learn the valley grows other things of beauty and a winner in any regal competition. Your qualities maybe said to partake of the variety of fruit which surrounds you. Such as the Roman Beauty, Delicious, and Pippin.

    To be selected for this honor indicates you have, quite unconsciously, of course, the best qualities of the aforementioned fruits. My congratulations to you. Enjoy your queenly role.

    Best wishes for a delightful Holiday Season.

Very cordially yours,

Victor A. Meyers
Secretary of State

VAM:cd

Dian Ulrich checks a guest in at the Cascadian Hotel's front desk. She was featured as a "new face" in the July 1959 issue of Western Hotel's employee magazine, *Front!*, as a switchboard operator. Ulrich soon became a front desk clerk. The hotel used a card system rather than a register. As always, service came with a smile. (Courtesy of Dian [Ulrich] Thompson estate.)

Bonuses were not always monetary in 1962, as this letter from James Reynolds indicates. Reynolds worked for Cole & Weber, a Seattle-based advertising company founded in 1931 (as Wilkins & Cole). After thanking Dian Ulrich for helping with the Washington State Apple Commission meeting, Reynolds asked her to use the enclosed check to buy Larry May some scotch and then to buy herself a hat. (Courtesy of Dian [Ulrich] Thompson estate.)

Wenatchee mayor Si Simenson (left) joins Cascadian manager Thomas Dupar in congratulating Dian Ulrich, Miss Western Hotels of 1959, at an informal dinner at the Cascadian. Unfortunately, the real trophy had not arrived yet, so a stand-in was used (the plaque on the trophy used reads, "Capitol League 1956–57 Lodge Team Sixes Cascadian 3179.") (Courtesy of Dian [Ulrich] Thompson estate.)

Ulrich was also given an all-expenses-paid trip to Vancouver, BC. As Miss Western Hotels, her duties included acting as hostess to conventions held at the hotel. When the official trophy finally arrived, Dian discovered that her name was misspelled on the plaque. (Courtesy of Dian [Ulrich] Thompson estate.)

Seven

THE END OF THE
CASCADIAN HOTEL'S LIFE

On Monday, July 19, 1971, a group of Delta Kappa Gamma delegates gathered for their scheduled meeting at the Cascadian. Upon arrival, they were shocked to find themselves greeted by shuttered doors and a sign stating that effective at four o'clock that day the hotel was "closed." The Cascadian had been struggling financially for quite some time. It was sold three times over a five-year period in the 1960s. Concerted efforts were made to reinvigorate business. In 1963, for example, the hotel began to serve Sunday brunch, providing what the *Wenatchee Daily World* newspaper described as "a new adventure in Sunday dining fun." Additionally, the opening of the Mission Ridge ski area in Wenatchee in the fall of 1966 helped occupancy levels. However, all of these developments only brought temporary economic relief for the Cascadian's owners. In accordance with Washington State law, the West Coast Hotel Company was dissolved on July 1, 1969, because of its failure to pay its corporation license fees, and it was clear to everyone that the hotel was also coming to the end of its life.

After the hotel closed, transformation of the motor inn happened relatively quickly. The Uptowner Motel opened in April 1972, with a business model that involved selling the refurbished apartments as 23 condominiums (the rules only permitted Washington State residents to purchase them). Although the weathered Uptowner sign remains, the motel has long since been converted into apartments.

The fate of the Cascadian's main building was more uncertain, and it took longer for plans to unfold. It appeared most likely that the building would be turned into subsidized housing for elders. At the end of November 1971, an application for government funding for just such a project was submitted to the US Department of Housing and Urban Development (HUD). With all the obstacles overcome, the Cascadian Apartments opened in November 1973, with 100 percent occupancy and an 85-person waiting list.

When the Cascadian was built, investors correctly predicted in the *Wenatchee Daily World* newspaper that it would host numerous conventions because it would be in a "position to invite and entertain many of the organizations, which, because of lack of accommodations, have been compelled to go to other cities." This image shows one of the hotel podiums (featuring an apple logo) being used by conference attendees. (Courtesy of the *Wenatchee World*.)

The 43rd annual convention of the Washington Collectors Association was held in Wenatchee on June 7–8, 1963. Hanging the organization's banner on the wall at the Cascadian Hotel are, from left to right, Kyle Younker, James Erickson (of Seattle), and Jim Phelps. Younker and Phelps were co-chairmen of the event. (Courtesy of the *Wenatchee World*.)

The 14,000 convention-goers in 1965 added $700,000 to the local economy. Numbers increased further in 1966. Lars Hendricksen, D.H. Leighty (of Spokane), and Gene Vanderhoff discuss plans for the 17th Annual Pacific Northwest Fertilizer Conference held at the Cascadian in July 1966. The conference drew field men and other representatives of the fertilizer industry and research officials from land grant colleges. (Courtesy of the *Wenatchee World*.)

Businessmen admire a collection of caricatures of local leaders decorating the wall at the opening of the newest meeting location in Wenatchee, the Cascadian's Civic Room, around 1968. The display includes a caricature (top row, second from left) of Royal C. Weinstein. After World War II service for which he received four Bronze Stars, Weinstein owned and operated numerous Wenatchee properties, including the Fashion Shop. (Courtesy of the *Wenatchee World*.)

The lobby of the Cascadian Hotel was filled with displays for delegates to a Waterways Conference. Of particular interest was the US Army Corps of Engineers display featuring the John Day Dam. Spanning the Columbia River between Oregon and Washington, the dam was completed in 1972. (Courtesy of the *Wenatchee World*.)

The Cascadian was a popular venue for club meetings. Mrs. Darrow Rorvik (left) and Mrs. Walter Cornehl admire the autumn-themed centerpiece that graced the speaker's table at the North Central District Federated Garden Club meeting held August 28, 1963, at the hotel. Cornehl is the new head of the district organization. (Courtesy of the *Wenatchee World*.)

The Wenatchee Hospital Guild held a number of their events at the Cascadian Hotel throughout the 1960s. Formed in 1948, the guild, which later became known as the Wenatchee Valley Follies Guild, still pursues its founding goal of raising money for local charities. In this photograph, three couples get into the holiday spirit for one of the guild's 1960s dinner-dances. (Courtesy of the *Wenatchee World*.)

All dressed up, Jeff Gerber watches as Gail Drewniany assists Mrs. Wes Hammond with decorations for a "Snack with Santa" brunch sponsored by the Children's Home Society of Washington on December 13, 1969. The event, held at the Cascadian Hotel, featured snacks, a program by dance students, and a visit from Santa. (Courtesy of the *Wenatchee World*.)

Wilfred Woods's father, Rufus Woods, became co-owner and publisher of the *Wenatchee Daily World* in 1907. He championed civic growth, including a 23-year campaign to build Grand Coulee Dam. Wilfred assumed his father's role in 1950, continuing the civic involvement, including owning the Cascadian for a few years in the 1960s. In 1997, Wilfred handed the reins to his son, Rufus, who carried on the family tradition. (Courtesy of Rufus Woods.)

Eva Anderson was one of the Cascadian's permanent residents until its closure in 1971. An educator and historian who believed in public service, she was elected to represent the 12th District of Chelan County in the House of Representatives, serving six terms, from 1948 to 1960. Sister-in-law of Rufus Woods, Anderson was the author of *Pioneers of North Central Washington*. (Courtesy of Rufus Woods.)

In February 1973, 18 months after the Cascadian closed, most of the hotel's furniture and linens were auctioned off at Colonel Jim's Gold Creek Auction House, in Woodinville. Some fixtures were left in the building, while remaining items were sent to other properties in the Western Hotels chain. One example is the silver-plated cream jug pictured here. The front of the jug is engraved with the trademark "W" signifying Western Hotels. By contrast, much of the flatware used at the Cascadian, such as this fork, could not be sent to other hotels because—as indicated at the base of the rear of the handle—it was stamped with the name of a particular property. Today, examples of these objects can occasionally be found in the archives of museums or libraries, or in private collections. (Courtesy of HJK.)

When the Cascadian closed in 1971, the motel inn was remodeled. It reopened in April 1972 as the Uptowner Motel, with a business model that involved selling the refurbished apartments as 23 condominiums. This 2012 photograph shows the weathered Uptowner sign painted on the side of the building, which remains the only visible indication that the motel existed. (Courtesy of HJK.)

Numerous items, from the heyday of the Cascadian's existence as a hotel, still remain in the building's basement. This original leather key fob, imprinted with the hotel's details and accompanied by a room key, dates from after 1961 when the motor inn addition was built. (Courtesy of HJK.)

This colorfully painted Cascadian "Fiesta" Central sign (stored in the basement of the Cascadian building) features the same apple motif as the lectern from the meeting room. It is all that remains of a Mexican-themed restaurant associated with the Cascadian. Several restaurants came and went in the lounge area of the hotel. (Courtesy of HJK.)

This is the original water tank for the Cascadian hotel. It is located in the basement and is still operational. When the hotel first opened, and for a number of years thereafter, the water source for the hotel was a stream that runs under the hotel (the water was collected, from the stream, and stored in the tank). Today, the tank is connected to the municipal water supply. (Courtesy of HJK.)

Two Otis elevators were installed in the Cascadian when it opened in 1929 and are still in operation today. In the 1940s, Harry Mullikin was one of the elevator operators. Otis elevator company continues to maintain them. The current freight elevator retains its original elements. By contrast, the passenger elevator has an updated interior. The manual relay board is the principal power source. It is a three-phase 440-volt system, controlled by a breaker box with a mercury switch. The governor controls the speed of the elevator and prevents it from running away. The round counterweights on the top spin when the elevator is in motion. The spin increases with the speed of the elevator. (Both, courtesy of HJK.)

This hand-painted sign graces the door of a second-floor storage closet. (Note the spelling of miscellaneous.) Hand-painted signs were common throughout the hotel, and included one for the coffee shop, painted by "Joy." The meeting room lectern featured an apple motif, and one can still see, on that lectern today, the pencil lines used to ensure words were painted in a straight line. (Courtesy of HJK.)

This natural gas-driven "Chicago Flatwork Ironer," manufactured by the Chicago Dryer Company, was installed in the Cascadian when the hotel opened in 1929. When the hotel closed in 1971, the ironer was still operational. During the remodeling of the building, it was simply disconnected because it was too difficult to remove the equipment from the basement, where it remains today. (Courtesy of HJK.)

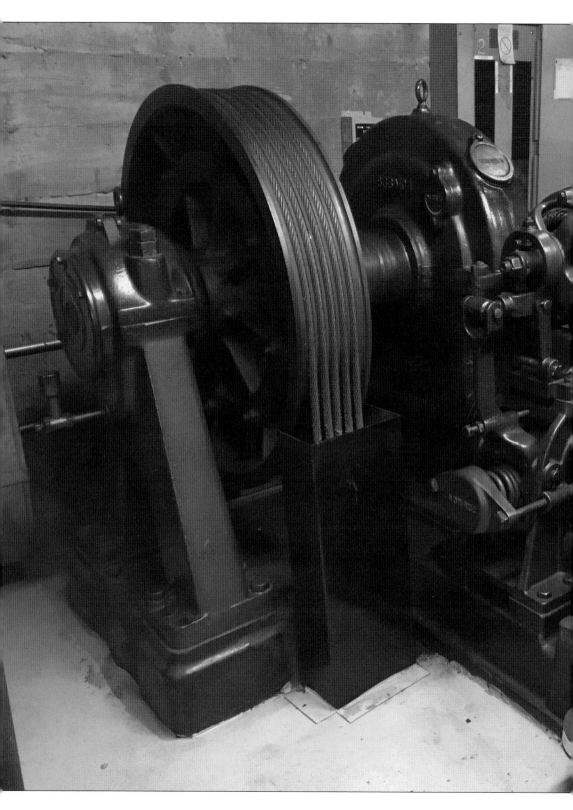

There are two drive and pick brake assemblies in the 10th-floor machinery room of the Cascadian building, one for each elevator. They operate like a drum brake on an automobile. Although there are five steel ropes, and four are for backup safety precautions. The elevator can be operated on one rope. Elevator safety is taken very seriously. At regular intervals, Otis runs a test that involves stopping the elevator at the fifth floor and then, with a technician inside, dropping the car in a free-fall to the bottom of the shaft. The landing can be felt throughout the entire building. (Courtesy of HJK.)

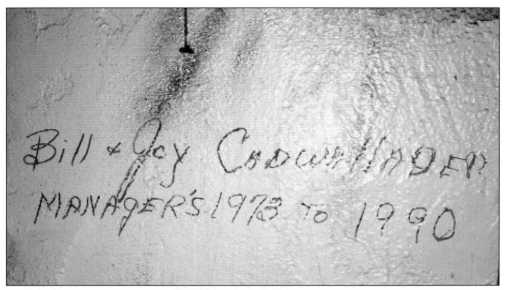

A poignant reminder that hotels are run by people, this handwriting is located on the wall in a storage room in the basement of the Cascadian. Duane Thomas "Bill" Cadwallader and his wife, Joy (née Lansing), were the managers of the building (in its post-hotel days) from 1973 through until 1990. They literally left their mark in this room that Bill used as his workshop. (Courtesy of HJK.)

They simply do not make letterboxes like they used to. This ornate mail collection box, connected to every floor of the Cascadian building by a chute, is the original one that was installed in the hotel in 1929. It is still used today by the tenants who live in the building. (Courtesy of HJK.)

This weather-beaten, wooden flagpole was installed atop the Cascadian Hotel in 1929. It still proudly sits in its original location. It is quite amazing to think that the hotel's opening ceremony featured a human spider that scaled the building and then brought his or her dazzling feat to a climax by performing a handstand on this flagpole, 127 feet up. (Courtesy of HJK.)

James Everett Stuart painted *Sunset and Moonrise on the Great Chief, or the Ruling Spirit of the Columbia* in 1894. Frank A. Dupar Sr. purchased this eight-by-five-feet oil painting in the 1950s. He hung it in the Cascadian's lobby, where it remained until 1968. It was then given first to Wenatchee Valley College and then (in 1985) to the Wenatchee Valley Museum and Cultural Center. (Courtesy of WVMCC.)

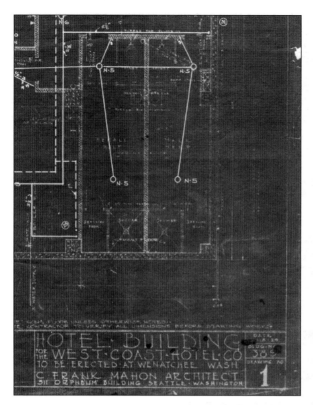

For all of the Cascadian Hotel employees like Elsie Parrish, their day would have begun here in the basement, where the dressing rooms were located. These blueprints, part of a collection currently stored in the building, show separate dressing rooms for the men and women. The basement also had a separate men's washroom, with terrazzo flooring, but no equivalent for the women. (Courtesy of Tryg and Barb Fortun.)

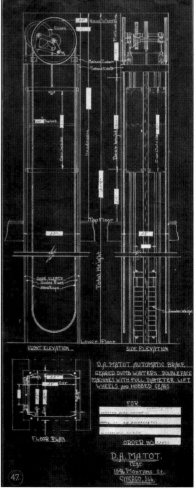

The Matot Company, formed in 1888 by Duffy Matot, in Chicago, manufactures and services dumb waiters to this day. They have long produced dumb waiters for the Otis elevator company. This blueprint shows the dumb waiter that was installed in the Cascadian in 1929 in order to carry food from the basement kitchen. Matot shipped it to Wenatchee for installation by A.D. Belanger's construction company. (Courtesy of Tryg and Barb Fortun.)

The Cascadian Hotel blueprints depict the building from numerous angles. The renowned Seattle architect Frank Mahon drew them up. Mahon's architectural skills also gave blueprint life to the Hotel Hungerford in Seattle. Bearing many of the same architectural features as the Cascadian, the Hungerford was the vision of Earl Hungerford, who invested heavily in the hotel business in the Pacific Northwest. In the Hungerford, the Cascadian's investors found not only the right architect but also the right construction company: the Everett-based firm operated by A.D. Belanger. (Both, courtesy of Tryg and Barb Fortun.)

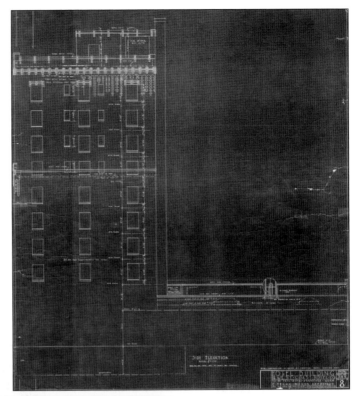

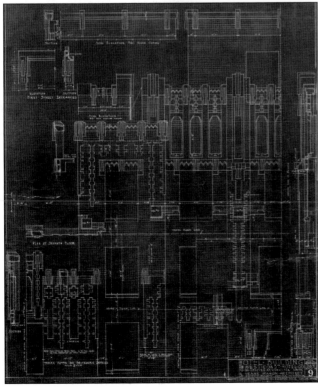

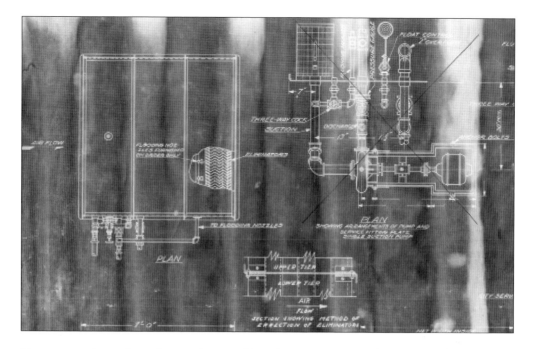

Using an apple analogy that readers would understand, the *Daily World* observed that the Cascadian's air conditioning system, involving two air washers (one on the 10th floor and one in the basement), two exhaust fans (one on the penthouse level and one in the kitchen), and one roof-mounted supply fan, "resembles that of an apple washing machine with a large spray on the inside through which the air is forced." The supply fan brought air into the washers, from which emerged the fresh, washed, cooled air that circulated throughout the hotel before removed by the exhaust fans. Operating constantly, this unique system ensured a "complete change of air" in the hotel every 60 seconds. These blueprints show parts of the basement and roof air washer system manufactured by the Seattle-based Western Blower Company. (Both, courtesy of Tryg and Barb Fortun.)

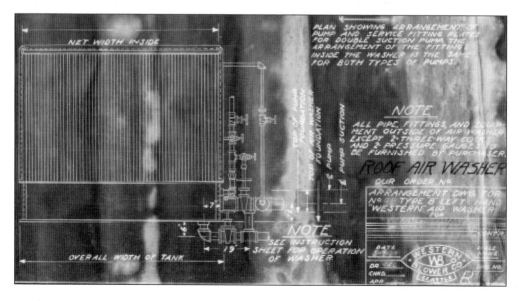

BIBLIOGRAPHY

Ackermann, Marsha E. *Cool Comfort: America's Romance with Air-Conditioning.* Washington, DC: Smithsonian Institution Press, 2002.

Blonk, Hu. "Recollections of Wenatchee's Old Cascadian Hotel." *Wenatchee World,* January 15, 1987.

"Cascadian to Be Outstanding Small City Hotel." *Wenatchee Daily World,* August 13, 1929.

"The Cascadian, 100% Air Conditioned." *Hotel Monthly* (September 1934): 53–54.

Gellatly, John A. *A History of Wenatchee: The Apple Capital of the World.* Wenatchee, WA: self-published, 1962.

"Ground Broken for $500,000 Hotel." *Wenatchee Daily World,* February 27, 1929.

Jakle, John A., and Keith A. Sculle. *America's Main Street Hotels: Transiency and Community in the Early Auto Age.* Knoxville: University of Tennessee Press, 2009.

King, Harriet. "The Man Behind the Megahotels." *New York Times,* May 8, 1977.

Knowles, Helen J. *Making Minimum Wage: Elsie Parrish Versus the West Coast Hotel Company.* Norman: University of Oklahoma Press, forthcoming 2021.

Lacitis, Erik. "Hotelier Harry Mullikin Got Big Things Done." *Seattle Times,* May 5, 2011.

"Popular Collegiennes—Superior Dining Service." *Okanogan Independent,* September 23, 1933.

Rader, Chris. "Block of Wenatchee Avenue Undergoes Change." *The Confluence* 29, no. 4 (Winter 2013-14): 4, 8-9.

Richardson, David. *Puget Sounds: A Nostalgic Review of Radio and TV in the Great Northwest.* Seattle: Superior Publishers, 1981.

Warner, Tracy. "The Night Nat King Cole Changed Wenatchee." *Wenatchee World,* March 10, 2000.

Woods, Wilfred R. "Talking It Over: Cascadian— A Building With Many Stories." *Wenatchee World,* October 26, 2007.

Discover Thousands of Local History Books
Featuring Millions of Vintage Images

Arcadia Publishing, the leading local history publisher in the United States, is committed to making history accessible and meaningful through publishing books that celebrate and preserve the heritage of America's people and places.

Find more books like this at
www.arcadiapublishing.com

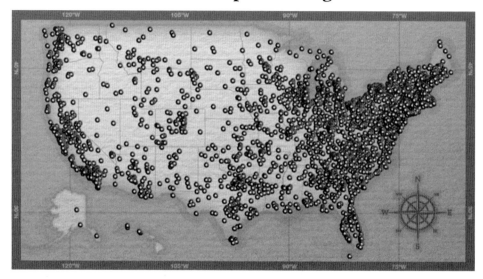

Search for your hometown history, your old stomping grounds, and even your favorite sports team.